MW01108425

The 12th Chair

Dr. Kevin McNulty

The apostles decided to fill the empty chair of Judas with one person.

God had a different idea!

Unless otherwise indicated, all Scripture quotations are taken from the *King James Version* of the Bible.

Scripture quotations marked ASV are taken from the American Standard Version, copyright 1901. Public domain.

Scripture quotations marked Amplified are taken from the Amplified® Bible, Copyright © 1954, 1958, 1962, 1964, 1965, 1987 by The Lockman Foundation. Used by permission. (www.Lockman.org)

Scripture quotations marked ESV are taken from The Holy Bible, English Standard Version® (ESV®), copyright © 2001 by Crossway, a publishing ministry of Good News Publishers. Used by permission. All rights reserved.

Scripture quotations marked The Message are from THE MESSAGE. Copyright © by Eugene H. Peterson 1993, 1994, 1995, 1996, 2000, 2001, 2002. Used by permission of NavPress Publishing Group.

Scripture quotations marked NASB are taken from the NEW AMERICAN STANDARD BIBLE®, Copyright © 1960, 1962, 1963, 1968, 1971, 1972, 1973, 1975, 1977, 1995 by The Lockman Foundation. Used by permission.

Scripture quotations marked NIV 1984 are taken from the HOLY BIBLE, NEW INTERNATIONAL VERSION®. Copyright © 1973, 1978, 1984 Biblica. Used by permission of Zondervan. All rights reserved.

Scripture quotations marked NIV 2011 are taken from THE HOLY BIBLE, NEW INTERNATIONAL VERSION®, NIV® Copyright © 1973, 1978, 1984, 2011 by Biblica, Inc.™ Used by permission. All rights reserved worldwide.

Scripture quotations marked NKJV™ are taken from the New King James Version®. Copyright © 1982 by Thomas Nelson, Inc. Used by permission. All rights reserved.

Scripture quotations marked NLT are taken from the Holy Bible, New Living Translation, copyright © 1996, 2004, 2007 by Tyndale House Foundation. Used by permission of Tyndale House Publishers, Inc., Carol Stream, Illinois 60188. All rights reserved.

Scripture quotations marked NLT 1996 are taken from the Holy Bible, New Living Translation, copyright 1996. Used by permission of Tyndale House Publishers, Inc., Wheaton, Illinois 60189. All rights reserved.

Scripture quotations marked YLT are from *Young's Literal Translation of the Holy Bible* by J.N. Young, 1862, 1898. Public domain.

ENDORSEMENTS

This book should become a must-read by every serious student of the bible. Kevin has taken a profound truth that he has personally walked out, and that has made him successful in over 60 nations in a span of three decades, and delivers it in a simple to read language so you can follow him as he does the works Jesus did, and greater. "The 12th Chair" is a book I will read and re-read many times in the days ahead, it has already become one of "my favorite books." T.L. is not here to read this powerful book by Dr. Kevin, so I would like to say what I believe he would say if he were here: "Bravo, Kevin, Bravo!"

Darrell Morgan, Pastor of Word of Faith Church, Apopka, Florida, USA.

Dr. Kevin McNulty's book "The 12th Chair" is tremendously inspiring, giving you a biblical foundation for what Jesus has accomplished for you, who He is in you, and that He desires to do miracles through you. Its truths are declared in the bible, and by reading this book you will be inspired to fulfill God's call on your life. I strongly recommend this book to young believers for a great foundation, and to older believers to have their heart stirred. Sit down, read, and rise up renewed in Christ!!!!!

Michael Schaefer, Pastor of Church Alive!, Albuquerque, New Mexico, USA.

I believe this book gives a fresh perspective on an important topic. It will motivate you to reach your greatest potential.

Peter Lowe, entrepreneur and motivational speaker.

The 12th Chair is wonderful, encouraging, uplifting and right on. Kevin reminds us that Christianity is supernatural, that we are supernatural, all of us-we are in Christ and He is in us. The world is waiting for you to believe that you can sit in The 12th Chair.

Ron Brammer, pastor of Rock Power Church in Des Moines, Iowa, USA.

First Printing 2013
The 12th Chair
ISBN 13 978-1-931-931729-13-8
Copyright © 2011 by Dr. Kevin McNulty
All rights reserved
Printed in USA

In the U.S. write:
Drs. Kevin and Leslie McNulty
Christian Adventures International
P.O. Box 15136
Daytona Beach, FL 32115
1-877-Tent-100 or (386) 252-9803
Website www.mcnultyministries.com
Twitter: Twitter.com/drkevinmcnulty
Facebook: Facebook.com/KevinEMcNulty

In India write:
Drs. Kevin and Leslie McNulty
P.O. Box 304 Guntur – 522004 Andhra Pradesh, India
Tel: 97010 11777 Tel: 0863 2254982

CONTENTS

MY MIRACLE MANIFESTOS

PREFACE

The drama of humanity unfolds for each of us in a different way, and each must come to his or her own destiny alone. Along the road, there are moments that will define us. There are glimpses of a future not seen before, nor even understood. It was a moment like this that set the stage for a new course that I have been traveling now for over 30 years. As captain of the Michigan State University tennis team, I had excelled in that sport for several years. Life was wonderful. I could see my future as a head coach at a major university with a career using the skill that had rewarded me in so many ways. There was only one question in my mind, but I did not expect the answer in the way it came. I wondered, *is this all there is to life?*

On a tennis court one day during the summer class session, I heard a voice say, "Read the Bible, read the Bible, read the Bible." This strange voice seemed to be coming from outside of me, yet I saw no one speaking to me. The voice was so strong that I stopped the match and told my

8

opponent what I was hearing. He said what was happening to me was not crazy and told me to follow him.

As I remember, we walked to his car and upon opening it I discovered hundreds of books and Bibles! He put several in a box and told me to read them.

This coincidence got my attention. I began reading the Bible, and whenever I saw him, I asked him more questions. After two weeks I realized that for some reason the Creator of the universe wanted to say something to me, but I had no idea why. I recall walking outside and, under an elm tree, opening myself up to Him.

I had read the Book of John and seen that Jesus was the focal point, so I connected with that and received Him as sincerely as I knew how. At that moment, a life change occurred. A cleaning took place that brought me to tears. Then a certainty entered me that I was absolutely going to Heaven.

This was unheard of in the religion I was raised in.

Four days later my defining moment of destiny happened. I was sitting in my University dormitory room when it looked like a strong wind blew into the room and started moving pictures on the walls. I got up to close the window, then realized that the window was already closed. When I turned around, I saw Jesus walk through the door and come up to me. He extended His hand and asked me, "What are you going to do with the rest of your life?"

I thought, *I am going to play tennis.* But when I opened my mouth, I said, "I am going to gather dead bodies and pump on old hearts!" This shocked me, and I exclaimed, "Who said that?" Immediately Jesus disappeared. I could hear

His voice, but I could not see Him. He spoke to me about several things and then told me which books in my room to get rid of.

After He had instructed me, I said to Him with all respect, "No priest or tennis player or family member has ever told me that You talk to them this way, and it is hard for me to believe that I am having this intimate conversation with You. Could You send one of Your guys to talk to me in the morning when I eat breakfast at 7 . . . someone with flesh and blood that I can relate to better?"

I went to bed and, as always, went down at 7 a.m. for breakfast before work.

As I was eating, a man asked if he could sit down. I told him the table was open—it's a university table. He said he was sitting in another part of the cafeteria when Jesus spoke to him and told him to get up and to come and sit with me. He told me he was a minister and then asked me what I did. I don't remember the rest of what we talked about, but I do remember thinking that the conversation I'd had the night before was real. I thought, *Oh my, He knows everything about me!*

Is it possible to have a moment when you see a glimpse of your future? God foreknew you from the beginning of time and sees you complete, fulfilled, and wonderful. The Creator holds that picture of us before Himself every day. And He gave us Jesus as a model and example of what we look like in His dream for us.

It has been several decades since that divine encounter. A great adventure has unfolded that has carried me from the vast tundra of Siberia to the tropical forests of Asia, to Latin America, Africa, and Europe. My wife Leslie and

I continue to stand on simple platforms in open fields before vast multitudes of people from every continent. Others have estimated crowds in attendance ranging from 5,000 to 250,000 people. Over the years this has added up to standing face to face with millions of hurting humanity.

I am still amazed at the wonders I have seen when I read the testimonies of those who have experienced a transformed life or received a cure for illness that no doctor, psychologist, or man could heal.

A Muslim lady who lost her eardrum as a child when she fell into a river,
suddenly bearing witness to perfect hearing, is one of
23 cases in Kazakhstan that helped thousands discover
and believe in a living Savior.

A grandmother in Kyrgyzstan who had been in a wheelchair
for 40 years, and whose sons had never seen her walk until then, brought
tears to a tent crowd of 10,000.

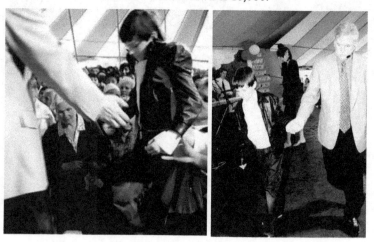

In that same meeting a boy born paralyzed was lifted over the heads of the
audience to the platform and walked for the first time in front of thousands.
What a witness of God's love for the Kyrgyz!

In Buenos Aires, Argentina, a young man blinded in a bar fight when a bottle was broken over his eyes, saw again for the first time since the incident, to the joy of the audience.

These and thousands of other testimonies must mean that our Jesus is alive.

I now understand what the meaning is of those first words that sprang from my spirit so long ago when Jesus appeared to me. The spiritual dead have come to life, and the hearts of believers have been pumped and recharged with hope, faith, and a fresh love for the living Christ.

Across the 23 newly-opened nations of Eurasia, we continue to raise up a generation of twenty-first century leaders in tent evangelism, releasing them to a potential they never realized was available. A great door has been opened in India to reach one billion souls, and we pursue it. We say yes to the countries who write and ask for ministry.

The Apostle John captured a powerful statement from Jesus: *"Because I live, you will live also. At that day you will know that I am in My Father, and you in Me, and I in you"* (John 14:19–20, KJV).

Is it now "that day" that Jesus was speaking of? I believe it is. Millions find themselves as I was, without an idea

13

of their own potential. Now my motto is, "Empower the dreams of people for the global advancement of the Good News." So many are not awakened to the great plan of peace, purpose, and power with which the Almighty has gifted them to fulfill the dreams and desires within their hearts.

When Jesus spoke to Paul, who was on the road to Damascus to kill Christians, Jesus asked: *"Why do you persecute me?"* Jesus identified Himself completely with the people who believed in Him. Jesus identifies with you and me as much as God identified with Him. Jesus said that it's hard to go against the grain. It's hard to fight a battle that is already done. You can't win against a resurrected man who can't be touched. What God has put in motion will stay in motion.

When will we know this reality—the reality of our self-portrait? The day that Jesus talked about, is today. The revelation in us is unfolding now.

What do you see when you look into the mirror? Do you see your weaknesses, your inadequacies, your imperfections? Or do you see what God sees? He sees you as the righteousness of Christ Himself. He sees you as more than a conqueror in Christ! We have an opportunity to look into the mirror of God's Word—the perfect Law of liberty—and allow it to transform us from the inside out!

We must not form opinions of ourselves based upon other people's opinions or our own failures. They do not define us!

See yourself as God sees you. His idea of you is as wonderful and glorious as the Apostle Paul wrote: *"But we all, with unveiled face, beholding as in a mirror the glory of*

14

the Lord, are being transformed into the same image from glory to glory, just as by the Spirit of the Lord" (2 Cor. 3:18 NKJV).

This wonderful nugget 'made into His image' is a noble goal. It is our destiny! Men and women are fulfilled more by goals than glory or gold. Understanding position is the first step to productivity.

Men and women who find a nugget of truth, either from Scripture or personal experience, tend to remove or diminish its supernatural nature. There is something in human nature that wants to control all truth and turn it into a religion. But there are dynamics that cannot be controlled.

Everything about Jesus is supernatural—His virgin birth, His sinless life, His miracle lifestyle, His substitutionary death, His resurrection from the tomb, and His indwelling presence in humans. He is offering His kind of life for humans to discover and walk in, but it comes at the price of not being comfortable.

Change is coming—let it come for the better. Change comes from crisis or revelation. This book in your hands is a revelation of God's dream for you. Let it become *your* dream.

INTRODUCTION

Two Russian grandmothers lived on their country's border with Finland. For sixty years they were never able to cross that border. When permission was finally given for Russians to walk freely into Finland, these two grandmothers slowly proceeded along their crumbling walkway, where wild grass had always grown between the cracks, into a foreign country.

They traveled 300 feet before stepping over the border into this unknown nation. Quietly they journeyed down sturdy streets free of trash, weeds, and cracks—all the while peering up at brick buildings unstained by coal smoke.

Tears formed in their eyes as they realized they had settled for a lie their whole lives. What their foreign neighbors had was so much better than they had imagined! They had lived as paupers but were told that they were queens as they survived on bread and sausage.

The story of these grandmothers gives us a picture of most of humanity. Most people are living in spiritual poverty, but all are invited to cross the border into the fearless life of one who takes his or her place in The 12th Chair! Are we living as spiritual paupers when we should be reigning as kings and queens of the Most High and Holy God? Do we feed on the crumbs in life instead of feasting at the Father's table as legal co-heirs of His Kingdom? What are we missing by not taking our rightful place in The 12th Chair—a place purchased and paid for by the precious blood of the world's Savior, Jesus Christ?

> **We only discover what unlocks our best when we ask the right questions!**
>
> **Answers wait for the questions to be asked.**

The Big Questions

Questions are the great stimulators. They cause us to think. God brings the answers to us when we begin reflecting on them.

Questions have an extraordinary capacity for finding answers. Often, asking the right question is more important than accumulating information. In His Word God tells us, *"Seek the Lord."* And when you seek Him with all your heart, you will find Him.[1] **Thinking, pondering, and contemplating are the first steps to seeking.**

When our questions rise to the level of God's potential for us, we step into a higher calling with greater possibilities. The right questions raise us to a life beyond success; they raise us to a better place—a life of significance.

---

[1] Jeremiah 29:13

17

If we don't understand this better place, we will live without powerful expectations. We will experience a lesser quality of life and a diminished view of ourselves and our God.

Humans need questions more than answers. God shows us the answer when we have the question.

So, what important questions must we ask? Here are some significant ones that we must answer to the satisfaction of our souls and minds if we are to walk in the light of our highest privilege.

- **Can we continue what Jesus began 2,000 years ago?**
- **What releases the Miracle Life within us?**
- **What knowledge will produce the dignity in us to stand tall like Jesus and see His results?**
- **Are Biblical miracles needed in the twenty-first century?**
- **Why did Jesus come?**
- **What is the revelation of God that Jesus brought?**
- **Why did Jesus come in a body?**
- **Who does Jesus say we are?**
- **What makes Christianity more than a religion?**
- **What do we tell the world that no religion tells?**
- **Can Jesus be the same in you in the twenty-first century as He was in a Jew in the first century?**

- Are Jesus' concepts workable or are they just a part of history?
- Are we living in the Gospels or in the Book of Acts?
- What makes us most like God?
- What are the gifts God gives every human being?
- How do we activate what we know we have?
- What brings dreams to pass?

We will find the answers to these questions on our journey through this book.

The Qualification

The Body of Christ has been qualified to sit at the table with Jesus and His followers. At the table you learn the keys of the Kingdom that Jesus gave to His Body to do what He did, and more!

What does sitting in The 12th Chair mean? It means we take our place as a voice for God's will. It means we are qualified to represent Him. It means we have been authorized to act in His authority. It means we have the same access to God the Father that Jesus has. It means we are highly favored and privileged!

It is God's Good News demonstrated that produces dignity in all human beings!

I would not dare approach the important subject of the miracle life if I were not supported by the following:

- **The Bible is a supernatural book!**
- **Jesus had a supernatural birth!**
- **Jesus gave us examples of supernatural miracles!**
- **Jesus experienced a supernatural resurrection!**
- **I had a supernatural encounter with Him!**
- **We are all called to do what He does!**

God is Spirit in Heaven, and He indwells flesh in the earth. This life that the Creator offers us by fusing us to Himself overrides all the limitations of our existence. Jesus introduced the idea that all things are possible with God (Matt. 19:26). For three-and-a-half years, Jesus showed what God in flesh can do. Then He made it possible for God to live in *our* flesh.

This Life Supersedes Nature

Have you ever stopped a storm? Jesus did. In a boat when all others feared for their lives, He spoke peace and the winds obeyed! Over the years we have seen the power of the Name of Jesus in similar situations when storm winds threatened our events.

It is truly a wonder when the winds respond to that name. It happened in the northern desert of Mexico at a church roof dedication. We were suddenly pounded by a mighty wind and rain such as the people had not experienced before. First, the side windows began to rattle. Then the roof we were dedicating began tearing off, panel by panel, right above the pulpit. The people ran for the door and the walls. I did also, but Leslie stood her ground at the pulpit and commanded the storm to stop in the name of Jesus. After she said the name three times, the wind and rain instantly stopped. The roof was saved and we had a glorious celebration!

This Life Supersedes Medical Science

Have you ever healed someone of an incurable disorder? Jesus did when a woman with an incurable blood disease touched Him. Recently I had an amazing experience—celebrating with two lepers who had received their healing at one of our previous meetings, and had returned to testify of their wonderful experience. Both had obtained a Doctor's report stating that their leper days were over! Indeed, one of them, an eighty-year-old woman also received her sight back, to the amazement of the crowd. We continue to see the "incurables" touch Jesus when His Word reaches their hearts, and they walk away healed.

This Life Supersedes the Law of Death

Jesus saw the dead rise when He called Lazarus from the grave (John 11:43–44). Can this happen today? We've heard of it happening in numerous places in Africa and Mexico. During our ministry in Ivory Coast, we heard of a woman who died during the event and was put in a wheelbarrow to be taken back to her village. On the way home a sudden, unexplainable miracle happened! Her eyes opened and life came back into her body. She told her son to stop pushing the wheelbarrow—she was going to walk!

21

What does the world want? They want good news. They want a demonstration of that good news. They want dignity.

We have stood among the 18,000 Buddhist temples of Bangkok and watched offerings of appeasement being made continually to their unknown gods to keep bad things from happening.

Kevin preaching the Word on the grounds of the Khon-Kaen Buddhist Temples.

We have seen the Japanese in their Shinto temples trying to cleanse the sin from within by breathing deeply from incense-laden bowls.

We have driven by the long, candle-lit processions of people in Mexico on their knees in penance, making sacrifices to ancient statues in hopes that a dead saint would intercede for them.

We have lived among the Russian Orthodox who chant their ancient language in churches. They don't understand what they are saying, and therefore the rituals cannot help the people.

During fifty centuries of Hindu philosophy, a religion has emerged with over 10,000 ways to communicate with a collection of 300 million gods. We have seen their thirst for God—it is unmatched in the world. Millions of Hindus go down to the Ganges River in India with the hope that their sins will be washed away, but the water cannot wash out the stain of sin.

For years we have worked among ancient Islamic civilizations with their repetitious daily prayers. They are searching for removal of yesterday's stain of sin, assurance of today's answered prayer, and confidence in future heavenly salvation. Without certainty in their hearts of any of this, they struggle.

The world has seen the prayer wheels of Nepal that must constantly be turned, in hope that the gods will give attention to man's need. Their monks believe in reincarnation, so they endure their chosen life of suffering, hoping they will not have to suffer in the next life.

We will not take the time to tell of the mountain trek to the cannibals of Aurora in the Philippines, or of the pilgrimage across China, or of the work among European secularists. Without miracles it would be impossible to convince the people of the world of a living Christ. Christianity would become just one of many philosophies without the confirmation of truth that only the Gospel guarantees.

Come with us as we explore this miracle life that God has called us to. Come and find out who you are because of Jesus.

Then step into the supernatural lifestyle that God has given to us through Him. Leave the cheap seats, take your place in The 12th Chair at God's table, and enjoy God's best!

CHAPTER 1

The early church imitated Christ. Should we?

What did Jesus begin that we continue?

Can Jesus be the same in His Word as He was in person? What did the disciples see, and not see, in the Cross?

Are we living in the Gospels or in the Book of Acts?

I walked into a bookstore looking for a small New Testament. What I found were thousands of books on every type of religion, philosophy, and self-help technique that one could imagine. Man's quest for truth is commendable. But without a guiding star to point the way, mankind would soon be lost in a myriad of opinions.

Religion teaches people how to suffer.

God teaches people how to make the devil suffer!

There are so many cultures and so-called gods in the earth. How could the Creator, the true God, be justified to all people of all generations in His dealings with mankind? He chose to come Himself, reveal Himself, and pay a price Himself for all humanity. This way, He would be justified in His judgment of the world.

Emmanuel, God with us in human form, is one of the names of Jesus. It is the revelation of Jesus that is the only real division in this world of different ethnic, social, and cultural differences. He rests His whole Kingdom and future on His own identity. We see this clearly in His question to Peter in Matthew 16:13: *"Who do men say that I am?"* The disciples spoke of the common thoughts of men when they answered that some thought Jesus was another prophet, or teacher, or a reincarnation of past great men. But when Peter said what was in his heart—that Jesus was the Messiah, the Christ, the One sent from God to redeem His people—then Jesus had a truth that He could build on. He said this truth was the rock that the Church would be built on and that no power would be able to stop it.

Then Jesus went further and revealed the authority on earth that those who believed this revelation would have. Whatever a believer stops or starts on earth will be recognized in Heaven and enforced with Heaven's power (Matt. 16:19). *Jesus took the revelation of Himself and turned it into a revelation of mankind whom He would indwell.*

Our life is short and eternity hangs on the choices we make during this vapor of time (James 4:14). Who will be our model to follow in this brief earthly interlude before we meet our Master? We can trust Jesus Christ as our model. He is believable. He is a trustworthy leader and an example for the ages.

In the face of storms, Jesus spoke peace and all became calm. In the face of taxes, He said to go fishing and gold was found. In the face of lack, He spoke blessing over bread and multiplication occurred. In the face of devils, He spoke a word and they were cast out. In the face of corrupt governments, He remained steady while they trembled in His presence.

We are called to walk in His likeness!

Jesus is calling us to follow Him into this same kind of life that He had on earth. He came as our miracle model. He gave us the power to live the miracle life when He gave us the Holy Spirit. Let us discover what we have so we can be who we really are.

> **When we know what we have from God, we know who we are. When we know who we are, we know what we can do!**

Anthropologists spend billions of dollars studying our past in hopes of knowing our present purpose. For us who believe, our past is rooted in the creation of man by God. We are made in His image, after His likeness.[2] Therefore Adam, the first man, was without sin and was a perfect reflection of His Creator. Scripture says that Adam's son was born in his likeness, after his image, and he named him Seth[3]. This was the pattern that God wanted to use to create a race of people like Himself.

---

[2] Genesis 1:26
[3] Genesis 5:3

Does it really matter that we lift the standard of a life like Jesus? The apostle Paul tells us in his letter to the Roman church that the whole creation is longing for the revealing of the sons (and daughters) of God (Romans 8:19). I think the world has been waiting a long time, and this generation has the potential, knowledge, and equipment to really shine as Jesus did.

This gives us a glimpse of God's original dream—to start a family with the potential to walk and behave like Him. Adam failed. He disobeyed God and did not fulfill God's dream. But God sent Jesus, Whom Scripture calls the last Adam,[4] and He did not fail. Jesus is the model for us to follow. How do we model ourselves after Jesus? Do we wear long robes with long hair and beards? It is interesting that in the four Gospels the writers did not talk about His appearance; His nose, the color of His eyes, His muscles, His height, His posture, or His hair. This is how popular writers describe their heroes in the books written today, but the Gospels are different. They are full of His words and His wonders. He is our model in response, action, compassion, authority, wisdom, purpose and power. We duplicate Him through the power of the new birth. The new birth is the ability to become God's child.[5] To as many as received Him, He gave power to become the sons and daughters of God. Paul tells us to put on this new man that is renewed in knowledge after the image of Him who created him.[6]

---

[4] 1 Corinthians 15:45
[5] John 1:12
[6] Colossians 3:10

28

> ## All the potential of Jesus as the Son of God was placed in seed form in you as a child of God!

You might say that this is unrealistic. Man is a sinner bound to sin and can never live up to the standard of Jesus' example. Well, what do you say about your children? When do you as a parent disqualify them?

When reasonable adults decide to have children, they are not under some misguided notion that there isn't going to be any misbehavior on the part of those children. Before the conception process even begins, they are fully aware that many problems will come as a result of their decision to have children, but the relationship is worth it to them.

It would have been easy for God to create us without the freedom of choice, but how meaningful could a relationship of that nature be? God knows full well the complexity of what is involved in the process of our obedience becoming genuine, from the heart, rather than something motivated by the fear of reprisal. And He is willing to endure "whatever it takes" to see that happen. Who's to say that the wait doesn't contribute to the joy for Him? I'm persuaded that nothing else is able to satisfy His great heart.

PART 1

THE SELECTION

It was a time of great upheaval! It was a time of signs, wonders, and miracles! It was the birth of a new era!

Those caught up in the change did not fathom the depth of the revolution in thought, faith, and worldview that was quickly emerging. It was this new revelation of Jesus Christ being raised from the dead that captivated them!

After He rose from the grave, Jesus had appeared to His disciples for forty days, speaking of a new Kingdom. He had given them the keys and command of this Kingdom, and He had told them to go to the whole world with it.

We find this group of eleven handpicked disciples, along with 100 more early followers, deciding that they definitely were committed to this new way. They were not clear on exactly what to do, and the waiting in the Upper Room seemed too long, so they acted.

Their first act was to fill *The 12th Chair*. This was the chair that Judas Iscariot, the betrayer of Jesus, had occupied. There was much debate over this 12th chair. Who was worthy of sitting at the table with the eleven who had been personally selected by Jesus? Who would be a qualified representative of the risen Lord? They were looking for one body to sit in that chair, but God had already chosen a body since the beginning of time. Who was it?

Matthias listened with interest as the eleven Apostles debated the need for a twelfth. He had been one of the sev-

enty disciples sent out by Jesus for some practical training in preaching. He was as surprised as the others when
the devils listened to him and came out. He never thought
anybody took notice, and now his compatriots were lifting him up to the highest status. In the back of his mind
he wondered, was this really supposed to happen? Jesus
appeared to all of us on several occasions after His resurrection, but He never mentioned this. Is this how God
does things? Drawing straws?

Matthias heard the qualifications for the job, and he was
one of many who passed the simple exam. The idea haunt-
ed his thoughts: was he really God's choice for the 12th
Chair?

What happened a few days later made God's choice clear.
Historic changes were unfolding. One era was fading as
a new one blossomed. The sun brought the morning light
that day as it always had, but something besides sunlight
was falling from the sky. Tongues of fire filled the Upper
Room where the Apostles and the rest of Jesus' 120 most
faithful followers were praying. The holy fire rested on
each head as the third person of the Godhead filled the
room. The Holy Spirit filled them all and they went out
preaching, teaching, speaking, and proclaiming the good
things of God in languages unknown to them but understood by all the nations assembled in Jerusalem that day.
God had made His choice for The 12th Chair: it would be
the Body of Christ!

The Apostles thought the qualifications for the one to
occupy this chair were that he had to have walked with
them from the beginning and have been a physical witness to the resurrection of Jesus. Again, God had another
idea!

31

God breathed His Spirit into everyone who would believe in His Son Jesus, just as He had breathed upon Adam in the Garden, and he became a living soul. Millions were about to enter into perfect harmony with God the Father—the harmony that Adam had enjoyed before he fell.

We catch a glimpse of God's decision by His selection of Stephen the church administrator, Philip the usher, and Paul the persecutor of the church—as well as millions more who would soon be sitting in the authority of Christ.

The religious world claims its authority in the physical church based on historic succession. Many institutions claim apostolic succession from the first disciples for their authority. Was it Jesus' plan to start another man-made institution run by a few men that would start the cycle of corruption and decay over again? No! God had a better idea and very big plans for The 12th Chair!

PART 2
PUT YOURSELF IN THE RIGHT PLACE!

The very heart of this series of books is to answer this question for every believer: *Can we continue what Jesus began 2,000 years ago?*

We must start by finding our places as God's representatives, continuing the ministry Jesus began. This is the vital first step toward a life of constant miracles.

- **There is a place where nothing is impossible for you!**[7]
- **There is a place where sickness cannot stay!**[8]
- **There is a place where you are equipped with more than enough to answer every need of every good work!**[9]
- **There is a place where peace, dignity, and love rule in your daily walk!**[10]
- **There is a place where you do as Jesus did!**[11]

I have good news for you! You were designed to fly into a realm where all things are possible!

The Lord invites us to a place without dark clouds above us or mountains in front of us. It is a place where we do not struggle for every breath of air, nor are we tormented by our past.

---

[7] Matthew 17:20
[8] Isaiah 53:4-5
[9] 2 Corinthians 9:8
[10] Romans 14:17
[11] John 14:12

"With the arrival of Jesus, the Messiah, that fateful dilemma is resolved. Those who enter into Christ's being-here-for-us no longer have to live under a continuous, low-lying black cloud. A new power is in operation. The Spirit of life in Christ, like a strong wind, has magnificently cleared the air, freeing you from a fated lifetime of brutal tyranny at the hands of sin and death." (Romans 8:1-2, The Message)

Jesus walked in that place. He came to earth to be our example of how to overcome in the natural by utilizing the supernatural within us.

Example is not everything—it is the only thing!

I thank the Lord for the models of ministry Leslie and I have been able to witness. Each one marked us with a living example of Christ in the earth today. The most defining living example was Dr. T.L. Osborn. He was truly a father of faith to millions and an elder statesman of global Christianity. For 16 years we walked with Dr. T.L. Osborn across the continents of this earth directing events and preaching with him in nation changing adventures. His DNA became ours as we navigated difficult situations with governments, church leaders, businessmen, and the sick, hurting people of the world. We were deeply marked by him as He followed Christ. Many of the insights we have tested on the different fields of the world were learned at his table. You also are being marked by the inspiration of this book to lift your eyes to a higher gold standard of expectation. Jesus is inviting us to lean close to His side and hear His voice, see His wonders, and know His ways.

God has called us to live, not just exist. We live when we discover our purpose, our potential, our power, and our position. We are seated in Christ at God's right hand without shame, guilt, or inferiority, but with power and authority! We are co-heirs with Jesus to the Throne of the Almighty! Throughout these pages you will find the keys to living as one of God's anointed ones, one of His chosen—one of those seated in The 12th Chair.

What does the world want? The world wants deliverance from the emptiness of life. The world wants dignity based on self-worth and inherent value. The world wants a destiny—a greater purpose for living. The Creator is offering all three to every person.

The Apostle Paul discovered this place that Jesus had held. Even though he was not present at Jesus' resurrection, and he had not walked with Him on the earth, Paul took his place in The 12th Chair! He shook the world when he summed up the wondrous revelation of God's plan, as recorded in his letter to the Roman church.

*"For whom he did foreknow, he also did predestinate to be conformed to the **image** of his Son, that he might be the firstborn among many brethren.*

*Moreover whom he did predestinate, them he also **called**: and whom he called, them he also **justified**: and whom he justified, them he also **glorified**.*

What shall we then say to these things? If God be for us, who can be against us?" (Romans 8: 29-31)

The four key words of what he penned are these:

(1) **Image.** God has made each one of us who are born again into a new person on the inside. The image that God sees is the true picture of our new self.

(2) **Called.** When we experience the new birth through Jesus, we accept the unique call that inspires us with God's ideas for our life.

(3) **Justified.** We are legal. When we accept Jesus as our Savior, God justifies us. He sees us as if we had never sinned. He has already put the entire penalty for our sins on His Son, Jesus. And He has given us Jesus' righteousness—His right-standing with God.

(4) **Glorified.** When we are born again, God glorifies us by appointing us His ambassadors to the world. He gives us His name that is recognized in all realms with ultimate dominion, power, and authority so we can march into action and tell people His Good News.

In this series of books we are looking at four dynamics that release the Miracle Life within every born-again child of God. To help you remember these dynamics, here is an acrostic of the word *live*.

L = _Likeness_ — Our image; Jesus' example

I = _Inspiration_ — Our unlimited call

V = _Validity_ — Our legality with credibility

E = _Expression_ — Our action now

Discovering each dynamic concept brings us deeper into the daily miracle lifestyle that Jesus modeled for us in His ministry.

This first book, "The 12th Chair," unveils the "L" or "Likeness" dynamic. When we are born again, we are remade in Jesus' likeness, in His image. We must see this God-given image of ourselves in order to sit in the "The 12th Chair" and experience what God has planned for us.

36

Jesus is the model; the standard and example that we are to follow. Being made in His *likeness* is God's intention for humanity.

Jesus had three-and-a-half years to show us how to live and minister. Why did He only need a little over 1,277 days to establish the pattern for mankind? Some church leaders preach for 20 years to try and get their people ready for service, but Jesus wrapped it up in a few years.

He was confident in His finished work, called redemption.

He was confident of His Spirit in us continuing the training.

He was confident in the new nature we received from Him through the new birth.

He was confident of God's favor on us and our new right-standing that connected us to Him and God forever.

If we are to be like Jesus, how does that make us different from former generations? Can we protect ourselves from the mistakes of the past? We can, if we continue what He began and not what tradition, ritual, and failed human experience have passed down. The Gospel of Matthew, Mark, Luke, and John yesterday has now become the Gospel of You today. Christ in human flesh in the Gospels has become Jesus in your flesh today. Much of the modern church would think this is an extreme goal that is too lofty for humans, but how does the unseen God reveal Himself to humanity? God is revealed in flesh. There is too much wasted prayer for God to come down and reveal Himself. He will not. He is in Heaven with many won-

Finding the Right Chair

derful ideas, but He needs flesh to reveal those ideas. He needs a voice. Christ in you is what He needs. As I travel the world and speak to multitudes who do not speak English, I need an interpreter. My ideas are without power until they are heard, received, and acted on. In that way, I am like God. He needs a voice. This is an awesome responsibility that God has entrusted us with; the message that saves humanity! If we don't do it, God can't do it.The present religious systems that fill the earth do not bring life. Could it be that the Christian religion is unattractive because of the accumulation of rules, practices, and theories that have been added to God's pure Word? It is like the Mississippi River. Where that river spills out into the Gulf of Mexico near New Orleans, U.S.A., no one would ever put a cup into the water to get a drink. You would see and taste the sludge. But if you went to the river's headwaters up in Minnesota, you would find thirst-quenching, refreshing water. On its 2,000 mile journey, the river picks up all sorts of impurities. In the same way, two thousand years of recorded history have added a great burden to the new believers of this generation. Let's drink refreshing water that makes scripture come alive!

What did Jesus begin that we are to continue?

As the book of Acts opens up, it makes a defining statement.

> *"The former account I made, O Theophilus, of all that Jesus began both to do and teach, until the day in which He was taken up,"* (Acts 1:1,2)

In Jesus' day, the Jewish people had laws given by God. What did Jesus begin? More laws?

They had the words of the prophets. What did Jesus begin? More prophets?

They had rituals. What did Jesus begin? More rituals?

They had the temple. What did Jesus begin? More temples?

They had priests. What did Jesus begin? More priests?

They had sacrifices. What did Jesus begin? More sacrifices?

They had sacred writings of rabbis. What did Jesus begin? More writings?

They had sacred traditions. What did Jesus begin? More traditions?

They had rules. What did Jesus begin? More rules?

They had the standards of justice and judgment. What did Jesus begin? More judgment?

All these prophets, rituals, temples, priests, sacrifices, writings, traditions, rules, and judgments, were already in place before Jesus arrived.

The best measure of whether your idea, plan, or program is successful or not is by what it produces.

What did all this religious structure produce? *It produced a Pharisee*...a leader arrogant in head knowledge, who judged all who did not measure up.

God got tired of it and said, "That's enough! I am sending them Jesus, so they can see what I am like and be like Me."

Jesus came to reveal not only who God is, but who we are. Here are a few revelations that the Scriptures give us about who Jesus is and how much we are all like Him.

"[Now] He [Christ] is the exact likeness of the unseen God [the visible representation of the invisible]; He is the Firstborn of all creation" (Col. 1:15 Amplified).

Jesus began a new species of god-men. He is the first-born so we are born of His family and likeness in the image of His Father, who is now our Father.

"For if we have been planted together in the likeness of his death, we shall be also in the likeness of his resurrection" (Romans 6:5).

And when did our resurrection occur? The moment we were born again from death to life!

"...Nothing between us and God, our faces shining with the brightness of his face. And so we are transfigured much like the Messiah, our lives gradually becoming brighter and more beautiful as God enters our lives and we become like him" (2 Cor. 3:18 The Message). We go from faith to faith, from love to love, from adventure to adventure.

When do we become more like Him?

As we see Him here in this life, we are changed into His likeness in deed and word!

"Beloved, now are we the sons (and daughters) of God, and it does not yet appear what we shall be: but we know that, when he shall appear, we shall be like him; for we shall see him as he is" (1 John 3:2).

There is no 'if" in this verse. It does not say we qualify if we are good enough, if we pray enough or if we give enough. He has qualified us by His sacrifice, His blood, and His victory over Satan. The key is to see Him and practice His presence.

As He is so are we in this earth. Why do we keep pointing to what Jesus did, said, and what is recorded of Him in the Bible? Because He is the true picture of who we are. He has set the bar for what God's original intention is for the new creation, then He paid the price so we could fulfill the dream.

When shall we be like Him?

The beauty of our new recreated spirit is like Him. Now we work out the salvation He put within us so the world can see Him. The same Spirit that filled Jesus and raised Him from the dead now fills us and has raised us from a boring, empty lifestyle to His quality of supernatural living.

"This resurrection life you received from God is not a timid, grave-tending life. It's adventurously expectant, greeting God with a childlike 'What's next, Papa?' God's Spirit touches our spirits and confirms who we really are. We know who he is, and we know who we are: Father and children. And we know we are going to get what's coming to us—an unbelievable inheritance." (Romans 8:15–17 The Message)

41

What did Jesus begin? Jesus began true leaders. *"'Come, follow me,' Jesus said, 'and I will make you fishers of men'"* (Matt. 4:19 NIV).

Jesus is still calling out to people to follow Him so He can make the best happen for them. When it does, the world will want to follow those who follow Jesus. The world will follow us when we are like Him!

**What you are is what God gives to you.
What you become is your gift back to God.**

PART 3
BEGINNING WITH THE RIGHT END
My Personal Journey

My ministry began with a curiosity that led to confirmations. I felt like a scientist with a theory to prove! My first thought after being introduced to Jesus Christ was not that I would do what He did. It never crossed my mind that I would stand before thousands of people around the world as His ambassador!

Instead, my first thought after meeting Him was, *What a sinner I am! It's amazing that God wants to live in me!* My second thought was, *What a relief! I know where I am going! Heaven is real, and I am going there!*

The goodness of God leads us to repent (Rom. 2:4). My discovery of this goodness revolutionized my life. A week after meeting Jesus, I was shocked when I prayed for a man with a crippled hand and then watched as he stretched it out, healed and whole. I had never seen a miracle, but seeing this one gave me a great desire to see more.

It seemed right to me that if God was willing to reveal *Himself* to me, He would also be willing to show me the ministry He planned for me. Thus began a journey with many a twist and turn as I navigated my way through Bible schools, mission fields, and churches.

Something kept prodding me to want to see a living Jesus operating among men. What would it take to see Him do today what He did in history? I did not know the answer to that, but I was very eager to find out!

I believe it is that still, small voice of destiny that was lead-
ing me. It is that call from the depths of my soul that even
now drives me on to new peoples and nations. As I go, my
heart is overwhelmed by the plight of humanity and by
all its glorious potential. People live as slaves in darkness,
without a clue about the victorious position Christ has
made available to them and the God-given dreams they
can have.

How do we help these people living in darkness? How do we
reveal the living God to them? How do we go to the nations
and fulfill God's vision for the world? Why aren't more of
us going? Is it fear that holds us back?

Our fear of missing God can paralyze us and keep us from
the very activity that God wants us to be involved in. At
times, I have felt as if I have missed Him by whole countries! Yet I have never seen Him forsake me.

A life of miracles requires risk. A life of miracles requires
decision. A life of miracles is lived without fear of making
mistakes.

I believe the life that God offers us is to walk in the same
way that His Son, Jesus, walked—and to walk that way in
our world today with its unique challenges. Each challenge
is an opportunity to discover the God-solution and grow in
understanding of Him. Each challenge brings a supernatural answer, favor, insight, and experience that make you
wiser than before and more able to walk in God's ways.

God's salvation is free, but a miracle life is not easy, free,
or cheap. Living it will require your focus, commitment,
determination, faith, and total effort in the laboratory of
your life, *"so you may prove what is that good, and accept-
able, and perfect will of God"* (Rom. 12:2).

44

Do you have a dream that you are delaying? Is there a vision that you have stopped visiting? Does your destiny feel denied? I have learned that one of the great secrets of life is to just *begin*. I guess I could be accused of beginning too many projects, too many buildings, too many countries, too many books, too many events, and too many enterprises. Let me just say that if I am to fall on my face, at least I know that I will fall forward, and that is progress.

When I began the global ministry, I had two part-time jobs and attended Bible school full-time in Valley Forge, Pennsylvania, U.S.A., but the secret was the passion to begin the ministry. One day the school had a guest come with a list of all the opportunities available in the world. I looked at the list, looked at the fifty dollars in my bank account, and decided I could make it as far as the Nevada desert in the western U.S.A. where the Paiute Indians were considered a mission field.

The school said I needed $500 and a car in three weeks, and I told them I would have them. A few nights later I was watching Christian TV with my mother. I thought I heard a voice say to give the fifty dollars I had to the preacher on TV. I said "NO! I need the fifty dollars more than he does!" I thought about it the next day and decided that if it was God who said to give, then there would be a blessing in obeying. If it was just emotion saying to give, then if I gave my fifty dollars in faith with joy, there would still be a blessing. So I gave.

What happened next? Nothing. Nothing happened the next day, the next week, or the next ten days. But after two weeks I heard a knock at the door. When I opened it there was a divorced, single mother standing there who worked at the school. She handed me an envelope with $500 in it, saying she needed to sleep. For two weeks God had been waking her up every night and telling her to give $500 to Kevin McNulty. I asked her if it was a Wednesday that He first spoke and she said yes...the Wednesday I gave the fifty dollars! Well, that got me on my way to the desert and around the world, and I haven't stopped since!

Friend, begin with what you have toward the dream in your heart. Your hope is the greatest force to carry you through the shadows of the night in the light of God's glorious destiny for you. Make the most of every opportunity for doing good in these evil days.

Your desire to live the miracle life will cause you to stand before new mountains and face new giants. Some will look as big as Goliath looked to the Israelites (1 Samuel 17). The giants may look big, but when we have heaven's perspective, they all become small. Scripture says that this is the victory that overcomes the world: *our faith* (1 John 5:4)! Our faith sees a big God within us and small challenges in front of us.

Kazakhstan tent outreach

One big test in our establishing a mass miracle ministry came on the cold tundra of Kazakhstan with thousands of people, Islamic by culture, huddled night after night under a tent covered with eight inches of unusually early snow. After doing my best to present Jesus, I knew that a sermon was not going to change a thousand years of tradition.

So I made a deal with the people: Would they agree to lay down their past and accept Jesus as their Lord if He would do what no hypnotist, no mufti, no Imam, or no doctor could do? They agreed. Without loud speech or exaggerated movement, I asked the forty partially and totally deaf people in the audience to put their fingers in their deaf ears as a sign to the others that God would answer prayer that night for any problem, beginning with deafness.

I read a prayer that I had prepared, asking God the Father to confirm His Son Jesus to the Muslim audience. A parade of twenty-three people with deaf ears now hearing came forward to testify! It was a powerful beginning to a mighty change in the city. We spoke the Word, people acted on it, and the living God confirmed it!

You may face the enemies of fear, sickness, poverty, loneliness, betrayal, disappointment, and all else that hell may throw at you as you work to establish the Kingdom of God through faith in Jesus and His promises. But each victory will bring you closer to Christ and make you more effective for Him in this world!

Can Jesus be the same in His Word as He was in Person?

In wonder we read, *"The Word was made flesh, and dwelt among us"* (John 1:14). Jesus is the Word revealed!

The presence of God's Word *is* the presence of Jesus. It brings transforming and healing power with it. The Gospel is the power of God that produces salvation (Rom. 1:16).

"So Jesus said to them again, 'Peace to you! As the Father has sent Me, I also send you.'" (John 20:21, NKJV) Jesus said "AS." In the same manner. We are not second class citizens of heaven. When Jesus sends you as a representative, you go with His Word, and He confirms this Word as His own (Mark 16:20).

How can Jesus be the same in His Word as He was in person? He can be, as we permit Him to be! We allow His Word to be our authority. When we see the face of Jesus, we see the face of God as He wants to be seen.

THE ONLY JESUS THAT THE WORLD WILL EVER SEE IS THE JESUS THAT IS IN ME!

If Jesus were to walk into the room in person, would you do what He said? If you would, then treat the Word in your hand as you would treat Jesus in the flesh. Doing this brings Biblical expectation to the twenty-first century. His Book becomes no longer one of history but one of experiences to be discovered. You will see supernatural confirmation of His Word. This truth keeps us speaking to masses of people.

When Leslie and I were speaking to a quarter of a million people in Ivory Coast, it was impossible to see the edge of the crowd. But among those present were three demoniacs. They were chained to trees because of their wild behavior.

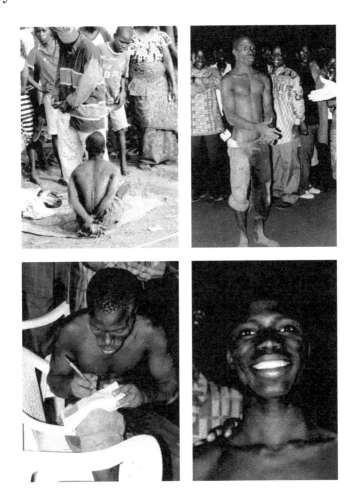

One evening, two of these demoniacs were unchained and brought to the platform. The Word had delivered them, restoring them to their right minds while sitting chained to a tree. On stage they demonstrated their sanity by speaking and writing normally—something they had not done in decades.

In that vast field of people, we could not personally minister to those demoniacs. But Jesus was there with them, because someone cared enough to put them in the presence of the Word.

In that atmosphere, Jesus could once more do His wonders through His Word.

People have said that I am a healer. Newspapers have written that the healing evangelist is in town. Am I a healer? Yes, in the sense that I am a vehicle carrying God's faith-energized words that produce healing power. God's words are the seeds that sprout divine life. And that life is the basic cellular foundation of our molecular makeup.

Today Jesus' healing ministry is the same as it was 2,000 years ago, except for the vehicle He uses. When Jesus was on the earth, He used His own voice. Now He uses the voices of His followers![12]

Other people say that I am just a psychologist and that I use mind manipulation to see healing results. I do not argue with them. When the mind is sick, all sorts of poisons are excreted that cause arthritis, hardening of the

---

[12] Acts 10:38

arteries, and hundreds of other problems in the body. John the Apostle wrote that we prosper and live in health as our soul or mind prospers (3 John 2). God's will for us is health, but our negative, fearful thinking can override His will.

When people hear the Good News, their thinking begins to change, and so does their chemical makeup. If I am a psychologist, then I must be the greatest psychologist in the world. First, I do not charge money for a visit. The meetings are free. What psychologist does not charge for his time? Second, I say you can walk away free of your disease in one meeting. What psychologist says only one session is needed? Finally, what psychologist in recorded history has ever opened a blind eye or a deaf ear? Where are the empty wheelchairs in their offices? Jesus is the Great Psychologist. But He is more than that—much more. And He lives in every believer.

We are given the privilege to write our own Book of Acts — the acts of Jesus through His followers in the twenty-first century!

PART 4

WHAT PEOPLE SAW, AND DID NOT SEE,
AT THE CROSS!

In the beginning, God breathed on Adam and Eve, filling them with His Spirit. Can you grasp the thought that when Jesus breathed on His disciples, their spirit was filled with God's Spirit?[13] Because we are born again of God's Spirit, we can now associate with God as Adam associated with Him: not as servants, but as sons to whom God has given dominion in the earth.

This was the beginning of a new era. They became a new species of being created in God's image. And they began a new way of life empowered by the Holy Spirit, with Jesus as their example on earth.

The world did not know what was happening. Satan did not understand what was taking place. His plan would soon become his defeat. When a Roman soldier looked at Jesus on the cross, he saw the rule of Roman law and power. When a Jew looked at Jesus on the cross, he saw a curse— for Scripture says, *"Cursed is every man who hangs on a tree"* (Deut. 21:23). When a Greek looked at Jesus on the cross, he turned away his eyes, for he considered himself above such things. No beauty there. No philosophy there.

The disciples did not really understand what was happening as Jesus hung on the cross. There Christ became our sin and we became God's righteousness on earth, enabling us to be His royal ambassadors to the world.

---

[13] John 20:22

They saw a man, but God saw all humanity.

The disciples saw hanging on a cross a man who had been judged guilty of a crime. They did not see the crimes of humanity put on that Man.

The disciples saw blood flowing from the head, side, and back of a man. They did not see the curse of sickness legally removed from humanity and put on that Man.

They saw a man lifted off the ground on a wooden beam. They did not see themselves lifted from the control of this world.

They saw the flesh of one man crucified. They did not see the flesh of all men crucified on that day.

The disciples saw a sign on the cross that read, *"King of the Jews."* But God had also nailed all the Mosaic Law to that cross and declared that Law fulfilled (Col. 2:14). Sin is no longer our master.

The disciples heard Jesus cry out, *"It is finished!"* They did not hear the High Court of heaven declare humanity free from the lordship of Satan, because Jesus had met the conditions of the law!

As Jesus hung on the cross, He was totally aware of His mission. Before His last breath He had enough presence of mind to ask for something to drink, so that all Scripture would be fulfilled. He was also thinking of others by forgiving the thief hanging next to Him and the soldiers mocking Him. It is amazing that as a man He was taking His last breath thinking of God's plan for His life!

Jesus had a reason to be so focused on the closure of that plan. He wanted to satisfy every jot of prophecy concerning the Messiah so He could say His last words without any concern for the future. Finally, He knew His mission was a success, and He declared, *"It is finished"* (John 19:30).

In actuality, all the Mosaic Law was fulfilled! He had walked under that Law as a man to meet its requirements so that we would not be judged today under a law we could not keep.

At that exact moment, God ripped the curtain of the Holy of Holies in the temple from top to bottom. Historians say that it would have taken six oxen on either side pulling on that thick curtain to accomplish this feat! That was God's way of attaching an exclamation point to Jesus' finished work. God was physically declaring that His presence would no longer be hidden from men. Now He had a right to dwell among people!

God was saying, "I will not hide myself from man any longer. I will dwell in them, and they will dwell in Me. I will remove their heart of stone and give them a new heart of flesh."[14]

---

[14] Ezekiel 11:19

You were on His mind

The greatest truth and mystery is the cross substitution.

It sets the stage for a new humanity to emerge from the ashes of sin, shame, and spiritual separation.

He did not die for Himself, He died for you.

He did not carry His own sin, He put your sin away.

He did not triumph over Satan for Himself, He did it for you.

He did not shed His blood so that He could be near to God.

You are made near to God by the shed blood of Jesus Christ.

He did not empty Himself on the altar of the cross to supply His own needs. He did it for you so you could enjoy all that God possesses and never suffer lack.

He did not have diseases of His own.

He took your diseases away and healed you.

The cross is not heaven's triumph over Satan. That occurred in heaven when he was cast out.

It was *your* triumph over Satan.

Jesus took it all for you. Jesus paid the price for you.

Now you are not a beggar before God. The basis for expecting answered prayer is found in the death of Jesus, who provided those blessings for you.

> **One does not discover new lands without consenting to lose sight of the shore for a very long time.**
>
> **—Andre Gide**

Until that moment, the Omnipotent One could only come *upon* men, because their spirits were not recreated. Now He can live *within* us so we can understand revelation and manifest Him on the earth!

How would you feel if you had just seen the death of the man who you thought would be your deliverer? Would it have caused you to lose your purpose in life? Two thousand years ago people thought Jesus was going to establish an earthly kingdom and destroy Roman rule. In one moment their dream was crushed. But three days later a new dream came alive again!

For 4,000 years of recorded history, God had led the Jewish people by the law and prophets. Now He leads His people by His inward presence. This is the difference between then and now. This is the new era we speak of!

In this new era, God plans to lead by His Spirit, who lives within every individual believer. This is more revolutionary than the revolution Jesus' followers wanted Him to lead. This is not just a changing of rulers; it is a changing of the ruled!

> **We are not called to study history.**
> **We are called to make history!**

PART 5

THEN AND NOW

A lot of confusion in the body of Christ today centers around a lack of understanding of the age we live in. Without understanding the times, we cannot take full advantage of the new contract between God and humanity that is sealed with the blood of His Son. It was not until that blood was shed and God's Spirit could re-enter people that the new covenant began. This also causes confusion for people who put the Gospels in the same light as the books of Acts and Revelation that followed them. The Kingdom was at hand in the Gospels, but the Kingdom had come after the cross and resurrection of Jesus. Under the Old Testament, sins were excused through ritual exercises, but in the New Covenant sins are removed by the blood.

In the past:

It was the ministry of Jesus in a Jew.

In the present:

It is the ministry of Jesus in you.

Do we dare imagine that we possess the same ministry and doctrine as Jesus?

Let us step up to a higher level in our thought patterns so we will not limit God's power in our lives. Let us go beyond reading the Bible as a history book to seeing it as a living, personal letter from God to us, to be applied to our lives today. Then it was the ministry of Jesus in a Jew. Now, it is the ministry of Jesus in you.

Our ministry is not different from Jesus' ministry; it is a continuation of His ministry, His doctrine, and His results! This new way of thinking will set us free from religion. When we realize that the Kingdom of God is within us and Jesus rules through us, then our posture and language are different, and our purpose for living takes on new dimensions.

In the past:

It was the ministry of God working through two hands, two feet, and one voice.

In the present:

It is the ministry of God working through millions of hands, millions of feet, and millions of voices!

The Body of Christ contains God's same multiplying seed that created the universe. Wherever we go as Christ's Body, we are reproduced. Put us in jail and the prisoners become Christians. Put us in a bad neighborhood and it turns into a model community if we allow ourselves to represent Him without apology.

In the past:

It was the story of history.

In the present:

It is the story of experience!

The Scriptures are not just something to be read; they are to be lived! They are the guidelines for a God-like life. They are not a rulebook to limit humanity's pleasure—they are a guidebook to enhance the pleasure of living without guilt, fear, lack, sickness, and all the other distresses of mankind. God's ideas are not to be put into a little box in your brain and taken out on Sunday morning for display. They are to be taken into the arena of life, where they will be shown to be superior to all other belief systems known on earth.

In the past:

It was the Holy Spirit upon them.

In the present:

It is the Holy Spirit in us!

We can look at the remnants of former moves of God in the earth and wonder why people continue such antiquated practices. Some women are not allowed to cut their hair. In some places, musical instruments are forbidden. Formality has replaced vibrancy. We must not allow the culture of church to replace the presence of Christ. In India one Hindu leader said it was a sad day when Christ was removed from Christianity in his country.

It is important to understand the times we live in and establish ourselves in the era that Jesus ushered in.

And the changes in this era are huge! No human being could have the indwelling presence of the Almighty until Jesus had purchased man's redemption with His sacrifice. God's Spirit could not live in us until Jesus had risen from the dead with new life to give to His followers.

All other spiritual leaders of history have died. They cannot give to their followers a life they no longer possess. Jesus rose from the dead, and He alone is qualified to give His life to others!

Today, breathe deep of the life He has given you, and recognize the unique position you have in the earth. Many a king and prophet would have given their places for yours!

In the past:

It was the Jesus of sacred history.

In the present:

It is the sacred Jesus living in me!

What a wonderful life has been given to us! We are not waiting for a special moment. We are not waiting for a special call. We are not waiting for acknowledgement from other humans. Redemption has already been purchased. We have a record in our hands of the life, death, and resurrection of Jesus Christ. We can celebrate Jesus' history, but we can also experience it again in our era. What God did to help people through Jesus, He is now doing through you and me!

I love history, and the history of the Church is rich reading. But I do not want to live in the past. We live in the present. What makes us relevant is that the Unchanging One lives through us—not a different Jesus, but the same Jesus who lived 2,000 years ago! We are not relic of days gone by, we are spiritual revolutionaries transforming the world through the truth of its Redeemer.

In the past:

It was Christ in Jesus Yesterday.

In the present:

It is Christ in me today!

The whole story of redemption rests on this one point: if the identity of Christ is not transferred to the believer, then Christ's presence in the earth is lost.

But the truth is, the same Christ, the same anointing, the same virtue and the same doctrine have been transferred to me!

In the past:

It was Jesus begun in one person.

In the present:

It is Jesus beginning in all believers!

I am inspired by the day I live in. I can think of no better time to be alive and no better time to see the Creator involved with His creation. Many acknowledge Him on Sunday morning and don't bother with Him the rest of the week. Most pay their respects and a few pay their tithes, but hardly any ever consider that they could walk as Jesus walked. Most people think such a life is only for the chosen few, the "special holy ones."

Is the life that Jesus gave up just for a few? Are the miracles He demonstrated just for the saints of old? Dare we think bigger in our generation?

You can imagine what Jesus was thinking when He said, *"I can do only what I see the Father doing. Without the Father working through Me, I am nothing"* (John 5:19–20; 14:10). *"But the Father works through Me, and I will work through you"* (John 14:20). Jesus could see that one body could do only so much.

He evaluated, "I am limited to this one body and one country, but now through you I will be unlimited. All things are possible for Me as I walk the streets of Israel, but soon all things will be possible through you on the streets of the world!"

"The works that I did you will do also, and even greater works than these. They will be greater as you go farther than I could go. You will touch more than I touched. More will hear your words than heard Me in this body."[15] Jesus has confidence in us, that we will walk as He walked wherever we find ourselves. Today is our day!

In the past:

It was the Bible description of the past.

In the present:

It is the Bible experience and action of the present!

Before the Cross, the Bible described the occasional great man or woman of God. But after the Cross, we who follow Jesus all have God living, breathing, and walking in us. It is only when we have this difference deeply rooted in

---

[15] John 14:12, author paraphrase

our belief system that we can experience the distinction of living the life of Christ on earth. No generation can live on stories of the past.

God has no grandchildren—He only has children! Experiences like those we read about in the Bible are not just for people with official titles. Rather, God titles each one of us. He calls us Son or Daughter. We are a royal priesthood, citizens of heaven, and ambassadors of the Mighty One!

Every believer who is filled with God's Spirit can be a person of action—walking in Christ's footsteps and doing what He did. Every person born of God can give voice to the truth of God's Word, and the Lord will confirm that Word with signs following!

In the past:

It was revelation.

In the present:

It is manifestation!

We get a *wow* out of all revelations! We are lifted to the highest places in our hearts and thoughts by understanding things we haven't seen before. We get thirsty for more of God's Word when a new revelation burns in our hearts.

That is wonderful, but there is so much more. As we step out into the miracle life, we are taken out of the classroom and put into the arena of life. We are privileged to see God on earth. We do not have to wait until heaven. Now, that is real living! That is the manifestation of His claim to be with us!

In the past:

It was Jesus, the example of God in human flesh.

In the present:

It is His reality in our flesh!

The Word says we are made in God's likeness. Jesus was the example of man made in the image of God. We talk about behaving like Jesus, and we ask, "What would Jesus do?" But let us go beyond that and allow Him to be Jesus in our flesh. He is determined to do His will through His flesh, and we are His flesh today! We are His conduits of blessing. You can be a small bathroom faucet or a great city pipe. God is pouring out His blessing from heaven 24 hours a day, but you decide the amount that will flow through you.

"My old self has been crucified with Christ. It is no longer I who live, but Christ lives in me. So I live in this earthly body by trusting in the Son of God, who loved me and gave himself for me" (Galatians 2:20, NLT).

In the past:

It was the incarnation of God in Christ.

In the present:

It is the reincarnation of God in believers!

Can we fathom being identified as a son or daughter of the Creator without puffing ourselves up as someone important? Jesus said, *"I can do nothing unless the Father does the work through Me"* (John 5:19). So we can say now, "I can do nothing unless Jesus does the work through me."

But we add, "And He is doing His work through me because I am *allowing* Him to."

In conclusion, we recognize that the times we live in are unique. These are times of highest privilege for humanity if we believe the reality of our redemption in Christ. We will discuss that reality in chapter 2.

CHAPTER 2

THE CHAIR OF REDEMPTION

Jesus sidestepped the entire religious system and started something new!

What does the world want?

Religion or redemption: What is the difference?

What makes Christianity more than a religion?

What makes Jesus unique among all spiritual leaders?

As the disciples waited for something to happen in the Upper Room, there is no evidence that they understood the redemption that Jesus had purchased for them. It is not even mentioned until Acts chapter 15, when Paul visited the Church leadership in Jerusalem after a dispute arose over receiving the Gentiles into the Church.

If He paid for it I can take it.

If He died for me I don't have to die.

If He was condemned for me I don't have to be condemned.

If He took my punishment I don't have to.

If He bore my sins I don't have to.

The leaders concluded that there is no difference between Jew and Gentile. Today we can understand that, **if it is redemption** and not religion, it is for all. **If it is redemption** and not religion, it is for male and female. **If it is redemption** and not religion, it is for all nations. The chair of redemption is "The 12th Chair"!

We get a glimpse of redemption in what happened after Judas betrayed Jesus. Zechariah prophesied that Jesus' life would be valued at thirty silver coins.[16] (That was the price paid for Jesus' betrayal, and these thirty coins are what Judas threw back at the religious leaders. They used the money to purchase a piece of land called the "Potter's Field."[17])

It is amazing that the purchased field was where all the broken, unusable, worthless pieces of pottery were thrown. Now we see in this "shadow" in the Scriptures that these worthless things were purchased with the life of Jesus Christ!

Jesus has purchased all the broken and unusable people who are considered worthless by society. They are redeemed with His precious blood. *"Now where there is remission of sin, there is no longer an offering for sin"* (Heb. 10:18). When our sins are remitted, or paid for, they are no longer held against us. We are paid for in full!

---

[16] Zech. 11:12-13
[17] Matt. 27:3–8

What is the Good News for everyone?

To a mortal man . . . . .a picture of God.

To a poor man . . . . prosperity.

To a nervous man . . . . .peace.

To a sick man . . . . healing.

To a fearful man . . . . faith.

To an angry man . . . . .self-love.

To an ignored man . . . . dignity.

To an uneducated man . . . . knowledge.

To a rich man . . . . .purpose.

**Is Christianity more religion,
or something more than religion?**

69

PART 1

THE UNIQUENESS OF REDEMPTION VERSUS RELIGION

Our travels for thirty-plus years to over 60 nations have brought us to certain conclusions on what helps people. Religion cannot help you. It has ritual, tradition, and history—yet it has no life to offer. Religion has postured itself as the connection to God and requires you to go through various forms and rituals in order to keep this connection. The Good News is that there is only one mediator between God and man and His name is Jesus. *"For God is one, and there is one Mediator of God and of men, the Man Christ Jesus"* (1 Timothy 2:5). The idea that each individual is free to make his or her own connection with God frightens traditional religion. The simplicity of faith as the means of salvation seems like foolishness to the religious intellect. The mind of man demands personal work—however, God provided His own work for salvation.

Religion will not accept IDENTITY OF THE DIVINE GOD IN OUR HUMAN PERSONALITY. That's why they killed Jesus; because He said God was His Father, making Himself equal with God. Religion always makes God holy and people unworthy. Here is the collection of Scriptural thoughts that links us to God as Jesus was linked to God.

1. **John 14:11 — Jesus said,** *"My father dwells in Me."* **He dwells in you and me too.**

2. **John14:17 —** *"The one who dwells in Me shall be in you."*

3. **John 14:20 —** *"I am in the Father, you are in Me and I am in you."*

4. **2 Cor. 5:19** — *"God was in Christ reconciling the world to Himself..."*

5. **2 Cor.5:21 — He became sin for us so we can now have His life and righteousness.**

6. **2 Cor. 6:1 — We are workers together with Him.**

7. **2 Cor. 6:16.** —*"I will dwell in you and you will dwell in Me."*

In conclusion, everything God has, He put in you!

Religion and Redemption, The Different Responses

The common thread of most religions is creation. As Christians, we call people to this common origin of God's image. From this point we can discover what "being made in the image of God" really means.

Religion has a different response to problems than redemption.

For example, a woman caught in adultery (John 8:3-8). Religion demanded the penalty of law which is death, and Jesus offered something better; forgiveness.

There was a demonized man with a legion of demons (Luke 8:26-36). Religion isolated him from society. Jesus had a better way and restored him to his right mind and used him as a representative.

We also see a sick man waiting by the pool of Bethesda for 38 years to be healed (John 5:1-18). Religion was upset because he was healed on the wrong day, but Jesus had a better idea and lifted him. Redemption brings healing every day to everyone.

71

People crave to immerse their lives into a cause greater than themselves. People look for something that will give self-value, purpose, and significance. People are on a quest for identity. Energy will be put into some cause if they do not sink their teeth into the cause of Christ. In the 1920's women were identifying with the right to vote. A man in the 1930's was wanting a right to work. In the 1950's men and women marched for civil rights. Our greatest rights are a right to self-dignity, self-esteem, and self-worth. Those rights were given when Jesus became sin so we could be the righteousness of God in Christ (1 Cor. 1:30).

To represent Christ means to live a life of Christian adventure. It is daring, supernaturally exciting, as you challenge yourself and the world. It is not a boring, static, unimaginative, or isolated life. You enter into the heart of Christ's victory. You can sing in the middle of conflict, for God is on your side!

Millions around the world who are hungry and searching will flock to hear your voice of hope and experience for answers to their prayers. They have been under the yoke of ignorance and can easily fall into the ditches of hate and fear along the road to destruction.

When you stand up, you attract the needy of the world. But you also become a target, because you rise above common thought. Do not be afraid if you are accused or hated because of your witness for Jesus Christ. Satan will shout from the shadows because he fears you. He will threaten you, but he has no power. Do not be surprised when the enemy comes against you. He hates you because of who you represent![18] You were destined to lead in a leaderless world.

---

[18] 1 John 3:13

In the early 1990's when we were pioneering church plants across Russia, we set a goal to launch five churches in the now open city of Kazan, which had a long history of being half Muslim and half Orthodox.

People were walking away from atheism to find identity in faith again. As I preached at the crossroads of several walkways, a large crowd gathered to hear this foreigner with new ideas of Jesus. Towards the end, a man let out a howl so loud that I took notice. He kept shouting "I am a Marxist! I am a Marxist! I am a Marxist!" until I could not hear myself. I told him to come forward. When he got to me, I asked him what his problem was. He said he did not believe my message. I asked, "Do you have a physical problem?" He said he was almost completely deaf from the machinery noise where he worked. To prove that God was with us, I laid my hands on his ears and commanded the deaf spirit to go. He began to hear and became very happy! At that moment, two police officers came up to remove me. They were going to be rough, but this man got between us and said, "Do not touch these people; I was deaf but now I hear." He was ready to fight the police as he shouted, "These people are of God. Do not touch them!"

The police changed their attitudes and politely asked us to leave so harmony could be restored to the area. We said we would go if they let us finish with a prayer. The crowd gathered and was saved. God got His harvest, and we saw His witness.

It is in the choppy waters of the ocean that a ship is declared seaworthy. It is in the air turbulence at 20,000 feet above the ground that an airplane is deemed structurally sound. It is after the trials and tribulations of life that one is recognized as enduring and overcoming. Ships were built to sail. Planes were assembled to fly. People were designed to face challenges.

A ship anchored in a safe harbor accumulates barnacles as dry rot sets in. An airplane parked in a hangar will suffer metal fatigue quicker than one soaring in the clouds. A person without a purpose greater than himself will never experience the joy of the challenge. That person will be weak in resolve and faint of heart in times of crisis. We must not shrink from the opportunities before us, but discover the unique way to overcome our giants.

This is why God gave us His kind of faith. It is not a natural faith that sees the obvious; it is a supernatural faith that sees God's hand moving in miraculous ways, with miraculous supply, and through miraculous coincidences.

In the year 2000 we took on the challenge of reaching the people of Kiev, the capital city of Ukraine, with the love of God in mass public prayers. It was an undertaking like no other! The government's new laws created enormous obstacles.

Two days before our event was to begin, the government illegally pulled all twelve of our permits. We were told that if we stepped up onto the platform, we would probably go to jail. The Orthodox Church even went so far as to bring in 5,000 pilgrims from former Yugoslavia to hold a counter-miracle event involving a mysterious holy head and bones of a dead saint!

They threatened to protest our event and burn down our platform if we stood up to preach. The police were told not to protect us. Instead, they were assigned to another organization that was told to have an event next to our site at the same time. Then the government threatened to close any security firm that would help us with protection.

Three of the five Christian organizations sponsoring that national event became so alarmed that they backed out. The national press was told that they must write negative articles against us or be shut down. Our lawyer said there was one clause in the new constitution we could stand upon if we proceeded with our meeting.

Based on that ray of hope, we opened the event. God then sent an angel to us in the form of Ukraine's ambassador to Germany. He was a believer who liked what we stood for, so he joined us that opening night. No policeman would shut down an ambassador! No protestor would burn down a platform with an ambassador on it!

First historic outdoor meeting testing the new constitution of the Ukraine, July 2000.

That night we began an historic test of the new laws of religious freedom in a new country founded on law, not on the whims of men, and we prevailed! Today one of the greatest revivals in Eurasia continues in Ukraine. I believe the seed of this revival was planted at that moment in time when believers stood in the open air of the capital and spoke out the voice of blessing on their nation. They were willing to face the challenge, and they experienced a miracle!

Whatever your challenge, remember as you walk by faith toward the purpose in your heart, more people are for you than against you!

Five Differences between Religion and Redemption

1. **Religion is** a "got to" way of life. **Redemption** is a "get to" way of life!

2. **Religion is** a door you must pass through in order to get into God's presence. **Redemption** is a door held open by Jesus that no man can shut!

3. **Religion is** man's attempt to satisfy a holy God. **Redemption** is God's attempt to make us holy by the sacrifice of a holy substitute!

4. **Religion is** a shadow of the things to come — it has no substance or power. **Redemption** is the reality of things to come — in the substance of our flesh and words.

5. **Religion is** form, ritual, tradition; an empty shell. It contains no life or revelation within. **Redemption** is the inner reality of the Kingdom of God in a temple of flesh. It needs no form, ritual, or tradition because the King Himself resides within!

Revisiting the question we posed in the previous chapter. If I were to take an empty glass, dip it into the Mississippi River at its mouth in Louisiana, and offer the water to you, would you drink it?

I have asked this many times, and no one has ever said he would drink it. But when I offer to fill a glass from the cool, refreshing headwaters far up north where the Mississippi begins, no one would hesitate!

In the same way, 2,000 years of picking up dogmas and rules from generations of people has made the Gospel unattractive, polluted, and no longer refreshing. Yet if we go to the headwaters of the stories in the Gospels, Acts, and the Epistles, we will be revived by a new taste of Jesus! The new message of the Good News—the Gospel—emerges!

Many people are caught in a religion without being saved!

The Bible tells a story of a man viewed as wonderful by people and God, but who was not saved. We see a man named Cornelius who was a good man but not saved;

- **a religious man but not saved;**
- **a man who was God-conscious but not saved;**
- **a real giver to people but not saved;**
- **a real prayer person but not saved;**
- **a man who saw an angel but not saved.**

An angel appeared to Cornelius and said, "God sees your hunger, God sees your giving and your lifestyle, BUT THAT IS NOT ENOUGH."

"Go get Simon Peter. He has words of life you need to hear so you can be saved." Cornelius had to hear and respond to words about Jesus to be saved. He was the first of the Gentile church to do so.

(1) "Now there was a certain man in Caesarea, Cornelius by name, a centurion of the band called the Italian band, (2) A devout man, and one that feared God with all his house; who gave much alms to the people, and prayed to God always. (3) He saw in a vision openly, as it were about the ninth hour of the day, an angel of God coming in unto him, and saying to him, "Cornelius". (4) "What is it, Lord?" And he said unto him, "Thy prayers and thine alms are gone up for a memorial before God. (5) And now send men to Joppa, and fetch one Simon, who is surnamed Peter. (6) He lodgeth with one Simon a tanner, whose house is by the sea side." (7) And when the angel that spake unto him was departed, he called two of his household servants, and a devout soldier of them." (Acts 10:1-7)

Our mission is to reveal the living God. Only when people see that God cares, loves, forgives, and wants to reveal Himself by revealing Jesus to them will they experience the God kind of Life.

The greatest prophet is the one with the greatest revelation. The revelations that John the Baptist brought were the first signal that a new era was upon us!

PART 2
REVELATION THAT ROCKED THE WORLD!

We see three new revelations from the man that Jesus called the greatest prophet, John the Baptist: *"Behold the Lamb of God, which taketh away the sin of the world."*[19]

(1) Jesus is the Lamb; therefore, no other sacrifice is needed.

(2) Jesus takes away sin, so sin is no longer covered over; it is blotted out.

(3) Cleansing is for the whole world, not one group or nation.

The first new thought John declared was that Jesus was the Lamb of God. John said this with hundreds of people and religious leaders looking on. The religious leaders thought John was out of his mind. They had killed animals for thousands of years to please God. They also were in control of the lambs that were slaughtered each day at the temple to cover over the sins of the people. So if there were going to be no more killing of lambs, then there would be no more need for sacrifices. If there were no sacrifices, then there would be no need for the priesthood.

If there were no need for the priesthood, then they would be out of a lucrative job! John was proclaiming that their jobs were being phased out! Jesus was handing them their resignation slips, because they no longer served any pur-

---

[19] John 1:29

pose in His new Kingdom! The new priesthood is a priesthood of every believer. Jesus would be the only mediator between God and man. The result of the liberating priesthood means the priesthood of redeemed women as well. It has taken up to now for these ideas to come of age. Behind the scenes Satan was extremely nervous about this revelation. How could he shut down this message? He used the arrogance of a king and the shame of his mistress to try and shut down this message by beheading John the Baptist. But the revelation could not be beheaded.

John the Baptist is heralded as the greatest of all prophets due to that one world-altering statement that was recorded for us to read.

The second thought John boldly announced in John 1:29, was that Jesus was taking away the sin of the world. The religious leaders wanted to correct John on this. They thought he must have forgotten that sins could not be taken away; they could only be covered over. They thought he had forgotten that God would wink at people's wrongdoings, understand their weaknesses, and grant them yet another year without penalty. But religious tradition would never let the people rise above the status of sinner.

John was asserting something new. Sin would not be pardoned each year—it would be paid for once and for all! People were going to be redeemed—left without the stain of sin or the lingering guilt of being sinners. A new creation was emerging.[20]

Many theologians, and in fact most of the religious world, still think God pardons a sinner the way a president pardons a prisoner, setting him free without his having to pay

---

[20] John 1:12–13

80

the penalty. In reality, God did not ignore our sin—He sent Jesus to pay for it.[21] This act produced real freedom that religion cannot offer.

Humanity is now redeemed. Our debt of sin is stamped "paid in full," with no charge against us. And God has no memory of our wrongdoing!

The third declaration John the Baptist made in John 1:29 was that the Good News was for the whole world. This really made the religious elite angry! God is not a respecter of persons.[22] Religion likes to horde truth, keeping it to its own group of people.

The truth the early church struggled with the most was that God was making His gift of joining His family with total redemption available to *all* people of *all* nations. When John shared this, his fate was sealed. His head was doomed to be taken off. But the heads of the rest of humanity were about to be lifted up in dignity!

Jesus continued to demonstrate this new truth that John spoke of. As Jesus was departing the earth, it is mentioned in all four Gospels that His last words were to take the Good News to the whole world. It was and remains His number one priority.

In Matthew He said, *"Make disciples of all nations"* (Matt. 28:19).

In Mark He said, *"Preach the Gospel to every creature"* (Mark 16:15).

---

[21] 2 Cor. 5:21
[22] Acts 10:34

In Luke He said, *"Repentance and remission of sins should be preached among all nations."*[23]

In John He said, *"As the Father has sent me, now I send you into the world."*[24]

Long after Jesus' resurrection, His message to the world continues to be His chief focus despite continuous resistance from world religions. The early church record in the Book of Acts is proof that this goal was also that of the first believers.[25]

John the Baptist paid with his life for stating that this Gospel was no more just for one nation, but for the whole world.

Stephen the martyr paid with his life for announcing that this Jesus was ushering in a new day for humanity. Almost all the apostles paid with their lives as they worked to reach the world.

To this day thousands of men, women, and children have forfeited their lives by standing up and saying with conviction that Jesus was for everyone, not just for one organization, denomination, or nation!

---

23 Luke 24:47
24 John 20:21
25 Acts 2:38–47

Therefore, we must conclude that if what Jesus preached is the Gospel of redemption:

- Then it must be for all nations, for all time!
- Then it must be for both male and female!
- Then it must work the same for rich or poor, advantaged or disadvantaged!
- Then it must work the same in every generation!

PART 3

THE UNIQUENESS OF CHRISTIANITY

What Makes Christianity More Than a Religion?

Christianity says things no other form of worship says. It was birthed in a miracle and continues through miracles today!

If you are sinful, there is salvation!

If you are fearful, there is new confidence!

If you are sick, there is health!

If you have no hope, there is new expectation!

If you are alone, there is a new friend!

If you are empty, there is purpose!

Christianity Is Based on Amazing Facts!

The wonderful facts of Christianity raise us from nobody to somebody, from simple to wise, from weak to courageous. These unmatched facts become living realities in a person when that person hears and chooses to believe them. What makes us like God and not like robots is our ability to choose!

We can choose to see wonderful days ahead. We can choose to expect good favor coming our way. We can choose to anticipate everything lining up in our lives as we rejoice in our Maker.

The alternative is to live in fear. We can choose to fear that the economy will go down and take us with it. We can choose to fear that the doctor's reports of cancer, heart disease, or a thousand other diagnoses are the final word. We can choose to fear tomorrow and fold up. Or, we can spread our wings of faith and exclaim that everything will work out! The facts of our faith put us in the realm of God. Jesus said, *"If you can believe, all things are possible to him who believes."*[26]

God has given us the sacred right of choice concerning our future. He has also given us the wonderful power of faith to make our choice a reality. All people exercise faith every day! There is a difference between natural faith and supernatural. Natural faith is based on experience and observation. For example, we drive by faith, expecting the wheels to stay on our cars. We sit on chairs by faith, counting on them to hold together. We eat food prepared by others in faith that it is not poisoned by a crazy chef. And by faith, all citizens rely on their governments to print money backed by value that will not cause their economic system to fail and bring on financial ruin, as has happened to some nations. This is all natural faith. Supernatural faith given by God is the ability to respond to Jesus in what He has done and what He is doing. This faith is not based on past experience or cultural habit. It is a revelation with an ability to see the unseen as more real than the seen. When the disciples saw Jesus on the cross they saw a man bleeding, but they did not see that the blood was the final sacrifice for the sins of mankind. It took a supernatural visitation after the resurrection and new birth experience to understand this new perspective on life.

---

[26] Mark 9:23 NKJV

THE CHAIR OF REDEMPTION

In light of all this, are we so strange to preach and practice faith in the Word, a Word that cannot fail because God is the source? We believe, not because religion supports our words, but because a Resurrected Man has the ability to back up what He claimed. He will always stand behind His Word!

A resurrected man believes in the written Word.

He said to search the scriptures for they speak of Him (John 5:39).

Jesus told His disciples to go to everyone in the world and preach this Good News. The Scriptures say He went with them, confirming their words with signs, wonders, and miracles.[27] He validated their words because their words were in agreement with His words. With their facts in order, they were unbeatable and filled with joy![28]

Fact #1–Born of a Virgin

Almost all religions state that Jesus is a special prophet who was born of a virgin.

What does this mean?

It means that God chose to identify with people. He did not come as a big mean animal, or a giant fearful apparition from the sky. He came as a human, as the Word that became flesh and dwelt among us.[29] God will eternally identify with humans. Because Jesus was human, He is moved with the feelings of our weaknesses.[30] He is committed to

---

[27] Mark 16:15–20
[28] Acts 13:52
[29] John 1:14
[30] Heb. 4:15

us because He became one of us. He said as He was leaving the earth, *"Lo, I am with you always, even unto the end of the world."*[31]

Religion likes painting Jesus as a helpless little baby that needs His mother. That is not the point. The real point is that God will eternally identify with humans . . . He will be the only one in heaven with scars. It is a constant reminder of the price He was willing to pay to identify with you and me.

Because Jesus now lives in us, we are privileged to feel what He feels and see what He sees. When we were preaching in Bashkortostan, in the Urals, a blind woman came to the edge of the platform during the final prayer. It was late and I was leaving the platform when I turned for one last wave goodnight, and I saw this blind lady flailing her arms to try and find where the voice was coming from. I felt the compassion of God and went back up to pray. With just a touch, Jesus did a miracle and opened her eyes. Wow! When we identify with humanity's needs, we are Jesus on the earth.

Fact #2–Lived a Sinless Life

Have you known a person in your own life or in history that lived a sinless life? "No" is most likely your honest answer. Yet we say that Jesus led a sinless life.

Jesus' blameless life means He is qualified to take our place—to take our sins and pay the price for them because He is not guilty of His own. He is the innocent Lamb who alone is certified as worthy to take away our sins.

---

[31] Matt. 28:20

Fact #3–Miracle Lifestyle

Many people in history are said to have done miracles, but who has come close to the miracle lifestyle of Jesus Christ? There have been many philosophers and teachers whom people could say might be equal with Jesus. But when He came down from a mountain and healed the leper, He elevated His teaching from a theory to a demonstrated truth.[32] If He had died and not risen, then this demonstrated truth would have just been part of history. But the New Testament says He did rise. What does this resurrection mean for our lives?

It means that through us, He is the same Jesus releasing the same miracles. He is not a weaker Jesus or a distant, uncaring Jesus. What He was, He is!

After His resurrection He said, *"Behold my hands and my feet, that it is I myself: handle me, and see; for a spirit hath not flesh and bones, as ye see me have."*[33]

Fact #4–The Christ's Substitution

Of the four pillars of Christianity, God's creation, satan's deception, Christ's substitution and man's restoration, Christ's substitution is the most difficult concept to understand. We can possibly accept the fall of Satan as an explanation for the evil on this earth because no witness was there. But you must accept by your individual decision the truth that Jesus became your substitute on the Cross for your personal sins. History records that He did live on this earth and die on the Cross. But Christianity goes beyond history into the present purging of

---

[32] Matt. 8:1–3
[33] Luke 24:39

each individual believer's sin nature, substituting it for a righteous nature by this act of substitutionary death.

This miracle declares that the blood falling from the body of Jesus is the blood of the Son of God. This blood satisfies the Court of Justice in heaven that all of mankind's sins have been paid for. Therefore, all who call upon Jesus for repentance and removal of sin are washed and declared sin-free, as if they had never sinned in the first place![34]

Our minds can look at past events and say they could have happened. But our minds cannot look at Jesus' substitutionary sacrifice without bringing the past into the present. If Jesus was my substitute, then I must personally decide to accept what He did for me. God gives no free passes based on our heredity. We each become children of God by our own individual response to this dynamic fact—that Jesus died as our substitute, in our place.

Fact #5–The Empty Tomb

Jesus' empty tomb speaks of a **resurrection**. No other spiritual leader ever rose from the dead to confirm his teaching. Jesus' resurrection validates everything He claimed. It makes all His statements not just a part of history, but a part of today's reality for any who believe His promises!

Fact #6–Jesus Lives in His Followers

The greatest miracle of all is that the same Spirit that lived in Jesus, now lives in us.[35] As we hold to Jesus' words, He

---

[34] Rom. 5:9
[35] John 14:16–17; Rom. 8:11

makes His home in us.[36] Paul the Apostle penned that it is Christ in you which is your hope of glory.[37] This is the key to a glorious life, because you are joined with God now!

We are connected with Him!

We are energized by His Spirit!

We are empowered to do what Jesus did!

We are enveloped in His Presence—He will never leave us or forsake us![38]

Who in history can compare to the teachings, demonstrations, and mastery of God's hand like Jesus, the Christ?

---

[36] John 14:23
[37] Col. 1:27
[38] Heb. 13:5

Part 4
THE UNIQUENESS OF JESUS

In today's society, Buddha, Mohammed, Moses, Socrates, Lao Tzu, Confucius, and a host of New Age prophets receive equal billing with Jesus Christ. Scripture told us this would happen.[39] However, we must look more closely at the credentials of these people to see if they deserve that position.

Christianity is the only form of worship where the object worshiped lives inside of the worshipper. Jesus now lives in us. He has a life to give. He is popularly called a prophet today, but no prophet of history ever declared that he himself was God or was worthy of worship. The main subject that Jesus spoke about was Himself. He said, *"I am the way, the truth, and the life. No man comes to the Father but by me"* (John 14:6). And many other Scriptures speak of His identity with God. After the resurrection Jesus did not correct Thomas when he called him God.

"Thomas answered him, "My Lord and my God!"" (John 20:28).

As he was being stoned Stephen saw Jesus at God's right hand and called Him "Son of Man." *"At that point they went wild, a rioting mob of catcalls and whistles and invective. But Stephen, full of the Holy Spirit, hardly noticed—he only had eyes for God, whom he saw in all his glory with Jesus standing at his side. He said, "Oh! I see heaven wide open and the Son of Man standing at God's side!""* (Acts 7:54-56 Message)

---

[39] 2 Tim. 4:3–4

91

What makes Christianity special? If Jesus is a dead prophet, then He joins the list of many dead prophets with good teachings. But, if He is alive, then Christianity is the only form of worship that can be confirmed by its founder. He proved Himself unique when He performed His first miracle, and He continues today in proving Himself where people can hear His words.

In the darkness of this world, we need a North Star. We need a fixed point to guide us through the night. We need something that will not change. People change, denominations change, economies change, governments change, and religions change—but Jesus does not change. He must be our fixed point. He is the Alpha and the Omega, the beginning and the end. We can anchor our lives to Him and He will carry us through the night and the stormy seas.

Jesus is our model for life. He is our model for miracles, relationships, and ministry. We are made in His likeness with the ability to live as He lived. He is the only standard that will pass the test of time. Enjoy letting His example become your experience!

Jesus Christ is the only spiritual leader in all history who came back from the dead. Of all the great teachers, philosophers, and prophets, His grave is the only empty one!

The common argument is that Jesus' followers bribed the Roman soldiers so they could have His dead body. This argument lost its validity when Jesus started appearing for forty days after the resurrection, and when His followers started getting the same miraculous results. No one could believe the lie put forth by the religious authorities!

Jesus Christ is the only spiritual leader in history who performs wonders, signs, and miracles to give evidence of the truth of His powerful words. The founders of ancient and modern religions are dead and cannot confirm their teachings from beyond their tombs.

Jesus Christ is the only spiritual leader in history who is alive in the present. Right now He is working, walking, and talking in the current affairs of those who believe in Him. All other religious founders belong to the past and can only be a memory.

Jesus Christ is the only spiritual leader in history who shares His divine life with His followers. Christianity is God being in us what He was in Jesus 2,000 years ago. Founders of other religions cannot share a life they no longer possess.

All religions are concerned with the past. Christianity, founded by the resurrected Jesus Christ, is the only one concerned with the present. We do not have a blind faith, but a demonstrated one. My present adventure in seeing the living Christ in my world of sports was on a tennis court. A player came to me on crutches with his ankle in pain and severely sprained. The doctor told him he could not play for a few months. I told him to put this foot on my lap, and Jesus would heal it. After prayer I told him to jump, and to his shock there was no pain anymore. We had a wonderful time playing! Jesus is the same in the 21st century.

Can Christian ritual without the miraculous transform human life?

I attended church daily for 22 years yet was never transformed. I never took religion out of the context of history to see Jesus down from the cross and in me. Our leader is alive. He now lives in us, giving us the ability to do what He would do when we are faced with the challenges of life

93

and the mission before us. His Spirit within us inspires us with His thoughts. And those thoughts equip us to face our enemies of doubt, fear, shortage, sickness, and all the other evils that beset mankind with the same calmness, confidence, and supernatural demonstrations that He would use.

We are energized to follow His model of ministry and keep Him as our standard in changing times. Jesus is consistent with Himself, He is consistent with people, and He is consistent throughout the ages.

People talk as if there is a smorgasbord of religions that they can choose from, acting as though one is as good as another. They either have not been exposed to the uniqueness of Jesus, or they choose to ignore it. **How do we respond when Jesus says,** *"I am the way, the truth, and the life: no man cometh unto the Father, but by me"*[40]?

This is a defining statement that the resurrected Lord and Savior has made about Himself. Why would people feel that it does not matter who they believe in? Could it be that they see no difference between themselves and Christians? Oftentimes those who know Jesus act like those who do not know Him. They respond to problems the same way, criticize others the same way, get sick the same way, and express their worries the same way. The people around them see no benefit, no reason to become a Christian!

For example, every people group can make Jesus just another part of their culture rather than a dynamic source of life. I was once a guest preacher in a church in the United States with a foreign-born pastor. I noticed that amazing

---

[40] John 14:6

94

growth had taken place in this pastor's church—over five thousand people had joined the congregation in two years. This was very uncommon. I asked the pastor what the secret was to this rapid growth.

He stated simply, "I am not of an American culture."

"Is that all?" I responded.

"Yes."

He was from another country, but there are many foreign-born pastors in America whose churches have not seen such growth. I asked him to please explain himself.

He said he does not talk like an American. He does not try to fit in like a good American. He is not shouldered with all the cultural weight of proper conversation, so he speaks his mind freely to all and trains his people to be like himself, which they are.

This pastor portrayed two powerful examples to his people: equal love for all and a passion to reach everybody with the Gospel.

This sounds like Jesus who did not care whether He fit into the cultural restrictions of His day. He spoke the truth freely, and the truth set people free, so they followed Him gladly.

The Apostle Paul exhorts us, *"Follow my example, as I follow the example of Christ."*[41]

You cannot really follow someone unless you think like him or her. The Israelites followed Moses, and Scripture

---

[41] 1 Cor. 11:1 NIV 1984

says they saw God's works, but they did not know His ways.[42]

What happens when we are reconnected to our unlimited source?

God in us is the continual source of life. If we are unconnected, we are not taking advantage of sharing His power and supply with others. We are similar to an extension cord. The power in the cord is latent power. It is present but not seen or used until plugged into something that will put a draw on it. All the power that is in God is in us when we are plugged into Jesus. When we plug into others through our words of truth, then all the power of God flows through us to meet their needs, just in the same way as it flowed through Jesus when He was on the earth.

Jesus tells us to heal the sick.[43] One of the names of God is Jehovah Rapha, the Lord who heals. We go out to proclaim healing to the masses or to individuals, and we expect healing to occur. People receive miracles when they hear us. They say we are healers. The truth is, God is the healer, but He needs a person to conduct His healing power through. When we minister, it looks like we are healing the sick, but in reality it is God who is doing the healing!

Here is an example of what I mean. If my car was immobile due to a dead battery, I would take my battery charger out to the car and hook up the cables to the positive and negative terminals. When I turn the ignition key, immediately the engine would start, because a new source of power was energizing the battery.

---

[42] Ps. 103:7
[43] Matt. 10:8

You might say that I fixed the car or charged the battery. But in reality, I did not. All I did was connect an outside power source to a lifeless battery. When I stand before people, and they hear through me the words that God has spoken for them, then their minds and hearts begin to receive healing.

The medical field has changed in the last 30 years. It now considers that many illnesses have their cause in psycho-somatic origins. That means that their sources are in the thought processes of man. I agree! Many of today's illnesses are rooted in the negative, worrisome, fearful thought processes in a person. Negative thoughts release hundreds of harmful chemicals into people's bodies that touch the organs. One becomes sick of soul before growing sick in body. I would take it a step further and say that these negative thoughts are doors for demonic activity and strongholds, as we see in scripture how devils look for gateways into humans. Paul says that gateways are arguments and ideas. (2 Cor. 10:4-5)

On the positive side, focusing one's thoughts on the Word of God promotes health. God's Word offers the encouraging truth of His plan for you. His Word brings joy, peace, comfort, and a living dynamic!

Of course, God's Word also does what no human can do. No psychologist can open a blind eye. No doctor can open a deaf ear. No hypnotist can remove a cancerous tumor. But God's Word carries the powerful impulse of God Himself into a heart filled with faith and creates a dynamic miracle moment, unexplainable by human evaluation.

We are called to heal the hurting as Jesus did. We represent Him as He is, with all He has for mankind. He is not a lesser or weaker Jesus; He is the One we read about in

Scripture: *"How God anointed Jesus of Nazareth with the Holy Ghost and with power: who went about doing good, and healing all that were oppressed of the devil; for God was with him."*[44]

God is now with Him in us, doing exactly the same things He did then. Believers follow His pattern and declare what they see in the prototype of Jesus, the firstborn from the dead.[45]

I was fortunate to enjoy an afternoon in the Sistine Chapel in Rome. When Michelangelo painted the chapel, he did not do it freestyle, just splashing on the walls and ceiling with whatever colors he felt at the moment. No, first he constructed a model of the room and made detailed drawings of each corner and each figure, so his work would not appear distorted when viewed.

Jesus is our model. As we go out representing Him, we must look more closely at Him. Why do people have a distorted image of Jesus? It is because we are the only image they see! That image can bring life, love, joy, peace, and healing power to every person on the earth. But if we do not represent Him accurately, people will not see who He is. We must recognize and carry in our hearts this statement: "If you can get to me, you can get to Heaven!" We can say that because we represent Jesus on earth.

[44] Acts 10:38
[45] Rev. 1:5

98

What will reflect Jesus' glory and demonstrate His power to a hungry and hurting world?

Let us understand Jesus not as just another nice spiritual man, but as the Living God. And let us not see His Kingdom as something to be looked forward to but as something to be experienced *now*! We must take one more step to untangle ourselves from the system of thought that denies power to us today and makes us spectators, rather than players, in the arena of life. What will get us out of the bleachers so we stop acting as observers, critics, and reporters and start making life happen now?

> **All that God is, He is in Christ.**
> **All that Christ is, He is in me!**

CHAPTER 3

THE HOUSE CHAIR

What unlocks the Miracle Life within us?

Why did Jesus come?

What was Jesus' mission?

Is Jesus our model or our memory?

In government chambers around the world, elected officials sit in their chairs representing their people to speak on national matters. In God's kingdom, we have been elected and empowered to represent God in all things concerning the earth. We are God's elect![46]

We have been chosen, singled out, and appointed to the highest position in the land. God has cast His vote for us. The devil has cast his vote against us. We hold the deciding vote on how we see ourselves. Are we God's representatives? Or are we just ordinary people?

God has empowered us with miracle life. It was imparted to us at our new birth. This new life in us is the authority we have to stand in our elected office. If we do not release this power, then we are just empty voices in a house of

---

[46] 1 Pet. 2:9

doubt. However, when the miracle life in us is released, we stand tall in the chamber of God's chosen, taking our legal place as His voice of righteousness!

When you have an encounter with Jesus Christ and surrender your life to receive Him as your Savior and Lord, it is not just an emotional experience. It is not just a rational, intelligent moment of decision. It is not just a cleansing of your past and a passport to your future.

The seed of God has been planted in you in the same miraculous way that the seed of God was planted in Mary to produce the Lord Jesus. You have to say yes to His will the same way Mary did. She did not understand how, but she said, *"May it be done to me according to your word."*[47]

Peter described this phenomenon by declaring, *"Being born again, not of corruptible seed, but of incorruptible, by the word of God, which liveth and abideth forever."*[48]

The life of God birthed in you when you accepted Jesus as your Savior and Lord is the same life that Jesus received in the tomb when He rose from the dead. The seed that resurrected Him to a new beginning causes a new reality of power and purpose in you as well. His work is complete. Now He works through you on the earth with His miracle life.

What will unlock the miracle life in us? In the next few pages, let us examine four answers to this significant question so that this miracle life becomes reality for us.

---

[47] Luke 1:38 NASB
[48] 1 Pet. 1:23

As a result of discovering Who Jesus is, you discover what He has done for you.

As a result of discovering what He has done for you, you discover who you are.

As a result of discovering who you are, you discover what you can do!

Part 1

UNLOCKING THE MIRACLE LIFE WITHIN US

These powerful concepts are at the very heart of your miracle walk on this earth. Reflect on the answers to the following questions, so that an explosion of new reality can grip your soul and launch you into new heights in daily experience!

What Unlocks the Miracle Life in Us?

(1) Understanding that we are continuers of Jesus' ministry!

Now that Jesus has ascended from the earth, He has left us with the grand purpose of doing what He was doing. We have been entrusted with God's most important mission: saving His people! Neither angels nor the Holy Spirit has been given this role, but only we who believe.

What Unlocks the Miracle Life in Us?

(2) Knowing that Jesus came once in His flesh, but now He comes in our flesh!

We have become His voice, His feet, His hands, and His heart to tell the world that the price has been paid, and that humanity no longer need be enslaved to sin and separation from God. When we accept Jesus, He moves into our inner man with every piece of His glorious luggage, and He calls us His new home! I am no longer alone. I have a friend who will go with me to the farthest reaches of the earth.

What Unlocks the Miracle Life in Us?

(3) Seeing Christ's Life as our Life!

The Apostle Paul came to this conclusion after three years in the desert and composed these words in Colossians 1:27: *"To whom God would make known what is the riches of the glory of this mystery among the Gentiles; which is Christ in you, the hope of glory."*

Jesus is the One who really brought forth the redemptive reality that God has chosen to live in us. With God in us, it is not a tradition, ritual, club, or duty that motivates our choices. It is the living Christ, who has decided to get personally involved in our lives.

What Unlocks the Miracle Life in Us?

(4) Understanding Jesus not as our icon but as our example!

Jesus is not some remote God to be admired; He is a friend to be loved. He is not distant and removed from the cares of this world—He is One who will walk with me through the challenges of this adventure. He is not an unreachable, unthinkable entity of the next life, but a model to be followed and learned from in this life. Why do they call us Christians? Because we are like Christ. This is not arrogance or haughty pride. It is how we are equipped to save the world.

On Cebu, an island in the Philippines, we had many experiences
among the stick people who lived in houses perched on stilts.
We had a beautiful salvation of souls as seen above.

This life is not lived on a platform but in every day experiences. On the Southern Island of Cebu, Philippines, we had
conducted a mass miracle meeting in the center of the city
with marvelous results, while enduring sweltering heat.
The people saw that God would answer prayer. Late into
the evening we finally arrived home dripping from head to
toe with sweat and exhaustion, then falling asleep in our
chairs. An hour later we heard a bang at the door accom-
panied with laughter. When I opened the door, there were
four young men who had brought with them a deaf-mute
that did not know what was going on. These boys were
not like the four men who brought the paraplegic to Jesus.
They were laughing at the mute and at us. A holy anger
gripped me and I had each boy test the deaf-mutes hearing
and speech. Then I prayed, casting this spirit of infirmity
off him. Next, I forced each boy to retest their friend, and a
holy fear came over them as they saw that he was healed by
God. I had them all confess that what they saw was from
God, and to repent and give their hearts to Jesus.

Part 2
WHY DID JESUS COME?

(1) He came to show us who God is.

(2) He came to show us who we are.

(3) He came to lay down His life—putting off the role of Leader, Model, and Example to become our Redeemer.

He Came to Show Us Who God Is!

God originally made man in His image. But year after year, generation after generation, people have gradually lost the image of God. Humanity is like a photocopy machine that is running out of toner—each new copy looks a little less like the original.

Jesus arrived in a world that had been pressed into a religious mold, lacking a heart for the living God. In the Book of Isaiah it is written that God had grown tired of man's sacrifices. Man's incense offerings were a stench in His nostrils. Listen to what He says:

> "'I am sick of your sacrifices,' says the Lord. 'Don't bring me any more burnt offerings! I don't want the fat from your rams or other animals. I don't want to see the blood from your offerings of bulls and rams and goats. Why do you keep parading through my courts with your worthless sacrifices? The incense you bring me is a stench in my nostrils! Your celebrations of the new moon and the Sabbath day, and your special days for fasting — even your most pious

meetings — are all sinful and false. I want nothing more to do with them. I hate all your festivals and sacrifices. I cannot stand the sight of them!' "[49]

In these verses you can hear the Lord's frustration with all of man's attempts to communicate with Him without a heart change. God was fed up with the idea of religion and all the rituals, sacrifices, empty words, and loveless hearts.

Why Religion Fails to Deliver

The root of religion is the sense of lost connection with God. It is the sense of lost dignity in His presence. It is the sense of not feeling right when talking to the unseen One, yet knowing that there is a right and a wrong.

Religion has replaced the confidence of a forgiven past and an assured future in Heaven with a variety of works in ten thousand shapes and forms. We are addressing the root of the problem so you can see the fruit of a wonderful, harmonious relationship with your Heavenly Father—the kind of relationship that you may always have craved but thought beyond your reach. The Kingdom of God is at hand. It is within your grasp. It is yours for the taking!

How was the Almighty One going to make His Kingdom on earth? His only solution was to send His Spirit and send the King, Jesus Christ, and give humanity an *example* of Who God is.

The world has forgotten what God looks like. The world's religions have made Him into images of wood and stone. They hide Him behind walls and ceremonies and shroud His Word in mystery with their dead traditions. By comparison, Jesus came saying, *"'If you had known Me, you*

---

[49] Isa. 1:11–14 NLT 1996

would have known My Father also.'"[50] Jesus offers us a relationship with the Father like the one He had! Jesus told His disciples, *"For the Father Himself loves you, because you have loved Me, and have believed that I came forth from God.'*"[51]

Jesus is heaven's revelation of who God is!

Jesus amplified this idea to us in a noble way when He said, *"He who has seen Me has seen the Father.'*"[52]

What Options Did the Creator Have?

If He appeared as a giant, then we would only be servants.

If He appeared as a voice, then we would know Him only as a mystery.

If He appeared as lightning and thunder when we disobeyed, we would know Him only as a judge.

So He appeared as Emmanuel—**God in man**. It was the perfect way for us to understand Him.

However, some cultures have a very different understanding of God without having Jesus as the picture of God. As we ministered in one of the ancient capitals of India, it was like we had stepped back 4,000 years into a time of chaos and confusion."

---

[50] John 14:7 NKJV
[51] John 16:27 NKJV
[52] John 14:9 NKJV

Kevin and Leslie in Madurai, India

The temple grounds were the size of 30 American city blocks, with bronze bulls and vast numbers of golden figures and painted priests. Three hundred million gods were worshipped in the city. The traffic got so bad because of all the images blocking the streets, that a law was passed prohibiting the people from putting their idols on the roads where moving vehicles were continually being blocked.

"To continue this thought; on another occasion Jesus said, I and My Father are one."[53] Immediately the Jews wanted to stone Him. He asked them which of His good works had prompted them to kill Him. *"'We are not stoning you for any of these,'* replied the Jews, *'but for blasphemy, because you, a mere man, claim to be God.'"*[54]

Jesus was comfortable as God in the flesh. Are we as comfortable with God in us?

Jesus clearly claimed attributes which only God has. When a paralyzed man was let down through the roof because he wanted to be healed by Him, Jesus said, *"Son, your sins are forgiven you."*[55] This caused a great uproar among the religious leaders, who said in their hearts, *"Why does this fellow talk like that? He's blaspheming! Who can forgive sins but God alone?"*[56]

At the critical moment when Jesus' life was at stake, the high priest put the question to Him directly: *"'Are you the Christ, the Son of the Blessed One?' 'I am,' said Jesus. 'And you will see the Son of Man sitting at the right hand of the Mighty One and coming on the clouds of heaven.' The high priest tore his clothes. 'Why do we need any more witnesses?' he asked. 'You have heard the blasphemy.'"*[57]

So close was Jesus' connection with God that He equated a person's attitude toward Himself with that person's attitude toward God. Thus, to know Jesus was to know God.[58]

---

[53] John 10:30 NKJV
[54] John 10:33 NIV 1984
[55] Matt. 9:2; Luke 5:20
[56] Luke 5:21
[57] Mark 14:61–64 NIV 1984
[58] John 8:19, 14:7

To see Jesus was to see God.[59] To believe in Jesus was to believe in God.[60] To receive Jesus was to receive God.[61] To hate Jesus was to hate God,[62] and to honor Jesus was to honor God.[63]

Is Jesus God?

Consider Jesus' moral character, His creative power over disease, His resurrection, and His own words about Himself. If Christ rose from the dead, then we know that God exists. We know who He is and, greatest of all, we know that we are invited to experience Him personally. He does not just ask for worship—He invites us into a love relationship with Him.

> *"'Behold, I stand at the door, and knock: if any man hear my voice, and open the door, I will come in to him, and will sup with him, and he with me.'"* (Revelation 3:20)

---

[59] John 12:45, 14:9
[60] John 12:44, 14:1
[61] Mark 9:37
[62] John 15:23
[63] John 5:23

WHAT WAS JESUS' MISSION?

Part 3
WHAT WAS JESUS' MISSION?

- **Showing God in action!**
- **Showing God's original dream!**
- **Allowing God to be all He wanted to be in human flesh!**
- **Paying the price so humans could be filled with God again!**

The world is so hungry to see and know the living God. Once after I had preached in one of our Gospel tents in the center of the Ukraine, a very old, white-bearded Jewish man came alongside me. He grasped my hands with all his remaining strength and said in a hushed voice, "Thank you for introducing me to the Father tonight!" Then, glowing with peace, he hobbled off into the night.

Another time, the ambassador of a major Middle Eastern nation saw me reading my Bible in a hotel lobby in an Asian country. He jumped up, came over to me, and asked, "Is that a Bible?"

"Yes," I said.

Then, to my shock, this important man started to cry. He said he was going to hell!

"Why?" I asked.

He told me that his wife had turned him in to the authorities for having a Bible in the house. He had been thrown into prison and treated like a common criminal until he recanted his faith in Jesus.

113

I told him this was not the unpardonable sin. "You can come back to Jesus," I said. "He will receive you."

This brought great joy to his heart, and he prayed with great fervency in that hotel lobby. I gave him a Bible and he devoured it like a starving man!

Jesus introduced humanity to the Father. He said, *"'If you really knew me, you would know my Father as well. From now on, you do know him and have seen him.' Philip said, 'Lord, show us the Father, and that will be enough for us.' Jesus answered: 'Don't you know me, Philip, even after I have been among you such a long time? Anyone who has seen me has seen the Father. How can you say, "Show us the Father"?'"*[64] It is recorded that Jesus said, *"He who sees Me sees Him who sent me."*[65]

JESUS CAME TO SHOW US GOD. God has spoken to us through His Son, the express image of His person (Heb. 1:2). Christ is the image of God (Col. 1:15). Jesus came to do the will of God (John 6:38).

The ancient script says when talking of Jesus' connection to God, *"Who being the brightness of his glory, and the express image of his person."*[66]

John tells us, *"And the Word was made flesh, and dwelt among us, (and we beheld his glory, the glory as of the only begotten of the father,) full of grace and truth."*[67]

---

[64] John 14:7–9 NIV 1984
[65] John 12:45 NKJV
[66] Heb. 1:3
[67] John 1:14

These and many more scriptures point to Jesus' mission of revealing God the Father. As Jesus accomplished this, it caused great joy among the people, but incited great anger among the religious. The message of Jesus was that God will be in you like He is in Me, so you can be like Me. God came in the flesh like you and I to show us how we can be lifted to a new status resembling Him. This revelation of connection to God at His level is a wonder to be embraced and exercised on earth.

What happens when you discover that God is like Jesus?

The people of the world will change when they discover that the loving Father-God will relate to them. He is not inaccessible. He is not incomprehensible. He is not distant. When I look at Jesus, I understand God and I am not afraid of God. What is He when we discover Him in Christ?

God is . . . approachable!

God is . . . personable!

God is . . . forgiving!

God is . . . for us!

God is . . . not mad at us!

God is . . . healing!

God is . . . loving!

God is . . . delivering!

God is . . . offering relationship, not religion!

By coming to live among us, God has gone beyond the role of teacher, father, and judge. He has made us His personal apprentices!

> **It is the revelation of Jesus' identity that brings a revelation of our own identity and power!**
>
> **The only mirror that works for humanity is the one in which the image of Jesus can also be seen.**

In the Old Testament, the Almighty revealed Himself as the great *I Am*.[68]

Jesus served as an example of all that the Father was to the people, and He confirmed His identity as the great *I Am*.[69]

> **I AM what you need Me to be.** [70]
>
> **I AM your Comforter.** [71]
>
> **I AM your Provider.** [72]
>
> **I AM your Friend.** [73]
>
> **I AM your Healer.** [74]

One of the greatest proclamations and problems of religion is that you need something or someone between you and God so He will listen to you. This keeps people weak, unfulfilled, afraid, and poor for generations. It puts a yoke around the neck of the common man.

---

[68] Exod. 3:14
[69] John 8:58
[70] Matt. 6:31–33
[71] John 14:26
[72] Phil. 4:19
[73] Prov. 18:24
[74] Acts 10:38

Tradition says that you need a priest, a sacrifice, a temple, or a saint to stand on your behalf before your Creator. However, Scripture declares that there is only One Who stands at our side as our Advocate. That One is Jesus.[75]

The Holy Word declares that there is a blood-stained mercy seat in Heaven that constantly declares us **not-guilty and worthy** of being right with God—without sin, fault, or shame. We stand in awe before God's Word when we read:

"Seeing then that we have a great high priest, that is passed into the heavens, Jesus the Son of God, let us hold fast our profession. For we have not an high priest which cannot be touched with the feeling of our infirmities; but was in all points tempted like as we are, yet without sin. Let us therefore come boldly unto the throne of grace, that we may obtain mercy, and find grace to help in time of need."[76]

Now **you** can directly approach your Heavenly Father as a member of His family, not as an unwelcome guest. Jesus wants you to pray to your Father in His name.

I have been in nations where the majority of the people felt unworthy to personally go to the Father. They did not feel accepted in His presence because to them He has been portrayed only as a judge and not as love.

Some people have been marked in their minds from childhood with this impression. Others do not consider Jesus or His name adequate to make a way for them to approach the Father with their prayers, because the image of Jesus

---

[75] 1 John 2:1; Job 16:19, 21
[76] Heb. 4:14–16

that has been painted on their souls is of an infant in need or a dead man hanging on a cross.

Multitudes have concluded that the only way they can approach God is through Mary. These people think she can intercede for them because she will understand them and be merciful. They fail to consider that Mary was in the upper room with the other disciples waiting to be filled with the Holy Spirit.[77] Mary received the same Spirit as the disciples because she needed to be born again like every other disciple. Mary required a blood sacrifice to pay for her sins just as Peter, John, and all other believers did.

Religion's portrayals of Jesus as a man hanging on a cross, or as a baby, do not invoke a desire for relationship. These images do not foster the kind of love bond a resurrected Lord would desire. The Father's portrayal only as a judge in a high court does not summon up thoughts of a warm, accessible person.

Mary, portrayed with all her human qualities, is exalted by people blinded to their full redemption in Jesus Christ. They have elevated her to the position of God's spokesperson. She is promoted as man's arbiter with God the Father and our bridge to heaven. It is sad to think that Jesus, the Redeemer who is God in flesh, has been subtly replaced with someone whose name bears no power in heaven or in hell.

When I picture God, I am in awe of His personal love and attention for me. I stand amazed at His interest in my life. I sense nobility and dignity rise in me as I hear His call to go to the world of people, and I become aware of His need for me to help bring others into His family. I am ennobled with

---

[77] Acts 1:14

a sense of being right with God, redeemed, and cleansed by the blood of His sacrifice—Jesus Christ. Jesus has one hand extended into the hand of our Heavenly Father, and the other extended to us to complete the perfect bridge between us and heaven. My prayer is that people will grasp His hand and go beyond the rituals of religion to the reality of a relationship with our Redeemer.

Part 4

JESUS CAME TO SHOW US WHO WE ARE!

People have always had a self-image problem.

When God told Moses to deliver His chosen people, Moses said, *"Who am I?"*[78]

When God told Jeremiah to tell His Word to the nation, Jeremiah replied, *"I am but a child."*[79]

When God appeared to Isaiah, he was stunned, declaring, *"I am a man of unclean lips!"*[80]

When the angel of the Lord appeared to Gideon and called him a mighty man of valor, Gideon was hiding behind a wine press.

No one can make you feel inferior without your consent.

—Eleanor Roosevelt

All these people of God did not have the divine connection offered to us. What is the difference between being connected to life and being connected to religion?

---

[78] Exod. 3:11
[79] Jer. 1:6
[80] Isa. 6:5

Jesus was different. He was connected, comfortable, and confident in the presence of God. Jesus offers all humanity this same opportunity for divine connection.

- **It means to know God personally the way He did.**
- **It means a new response to circumstances the way He did.**
- **It means making a difference in the world the way He did because of the difference God has made in our lives.**

This is not old religious thinking. That kind of thinking does not paint such a hopeful, encouraging picture of a relationship with God. Religion has put God up so high that we can't reach Him. It has made God so holy that we must be unholy. It has made God so smart that we must be ignorant.

Jesus became a *model* of who we really are like. Jesus came to reveal what God really thinks and how He really behaves. For three-and-a-half years Jesus acted as an *example* and *model* for us. He felt that was long enough.

We accept this revelation as just another statement about Jesus. But this is *huge!* God the Creator had hidden Himself in shadows from His creation. But *now,* through Jesus, He has become accessible! This is a monumental thought for a human to consider.

Imagine staying in a foreign country. While there, you work on learning their language. You practice it, learning from a teacher and hearing examples of it every day. After three-and-a-half years you would speak it fluently. You would speak it like your teacher. If it was Spanish and you learned it in Argentina, you would speak with an Argentinian accent. If you learned Spanish in Cuba, you would speak with a Cuban accent. You can pick up the language of Heaven as well. You can talk like Jesus your teacher.

> ## The road to learning by precept is long, but by example, short and effective.
> ### —Seneca

The Bible says that Jesus' followers saw His glory, and they saw that He was full of grace and truth.[81] They observed Him. They examined Him. They really pondered Him. They came to be in awe of Him! This explains why in the end they walked away from their time with Him with such power. They saw Jesus for who He really was and is to us. That image got deep inside them![82] Even the religious leaders were astonished and had to acknowledge that Jesus' disciples had been with Him. Religion will never welcome or embrace a person identifying with God as Jesus identified with Him, without sin, fear, and doubt. Jesus saying that God was His Father stirred religious people to kill Him, because He made Himself equal with God. Religion always makes God holy and people unworthy. Scriptures confirm the divine connection:

1. John 14 — Jesus said, "My Father dwells in me"... We can now say, "in me too!"

---

[81] John 1:14
[82] Matt. 9:8; Luke 5:26, 7:16, 9:32; John 2:11

2. John 14:17 — "The One who dwells in Me shall be in you".

3. John 14: 20 — "I am in the Father, you are in Me and I am in you".

4. 2 Cor 5:19 — God was in Christ reconciling the world to Himself.

5. 2 Cor. 5:21 — He became sin for us now so we can have His life and righteousness.

6. 2 Cor 6: 1 — We are workers together with Him.

7. 1 Cor 6: 17 — "I will dwell in you and you will dwell in Me".

This all reveals that we who follow Jesus begin to look like Him. As we consider Him, we are transformed into His image and reflect His likeness. This is the key dynamic and central theme that makes following Jesus so powerful. He came to show us who we are!

Jesus invites us to experience life on His level. He said, *"And I, if I be lifted up from the earth, will draw all men unto me."*[83] Jesus is a lifting experience for us.

John dared to write of this elevated human dignity and experience this way: *"Herein is our love made perfect, that we may have boldness in the day of judgment: because as he is, so are we in this world."*[84]

He is not talking about the day of judgment in heaven. We have boldness now when we are judged by our feelings, our past, our weaknesses, and the devil. We are bold now because He is living through us in this world.

---

[83] John 12:32
[84] 1 John 4:17

Jesus said to the Father, *"As You sent Me into the world, I also have sent them into the world."*[85]

Every one of us can say that we have seen a great difference between the person that we were in the past and our current privileged status as representatives of the Eternal One.

For some like a man named Ruslan, the difference is quick and dramatic. He was a drunk from Kazakhstan who failed in his religion, his job, and was failing in his family.

One day after Ruslan had been on another drunken binge for several days, his wife Lubov had to go to work. In the street, a woman came to her. "I don't know why I came exactly to you," she said, "But you need to come to the Festival of Miracles in the yellow and white tent." This woman gave Lubov an invitation and the exact address, so she and her children came to the Festival. The next day they brought Ruslan, who was just coming out of his drunken binge, as well as Ruslan's mother and his nephews to the tent with them.

Because they had lived all their lives in the south of Kazakhstan, Ruslan and Lubov had only heard about the Middle East god; a serious god who punished all the sinners. Nobody ever told them that God loved them. Ruslan often visited the mosque and performed daily prayers, but nothing would help. The day Ruslan first came to the tent, he suddenly remembered a dream that he had had a few days earlier. In his dream he saw this very same park and the same yellow and white tent! Ruslan was afraid that God would not forgive him, a sinner. But in the tent he felt

---

[85] John 17:18 NKJV

124

God's love and forgiveness, and made a decision that he would spend his life with the Lord. "Praise God that He found me, cleaned me and put me on a Rock of my salvation — Jesus Christ!"

Ruslan and Lubov from Kazakhstan

They all attended the Tent Festival for the entire week, and all of the family received Jesus as their Lord and Savior! God revealed to them both salvation and healing. Ruslan's mother was a medical worker in a hospital, and once every six months all the doctors had to go through a medical examination. During her exam the doctors discovered that she had Hysteromyoma and needed treatment. It was at this exact time that the Festival came to their city. When she came to the tent the first time, she received her healing. Physically she did not feel a thing, but in her heart she received her healing by faith. After some time she went through ultrasound testing, and the

125

doctors found that her tumor had stopped growing and was getting smaller.

In the short period of time during the Tent Festival, this family's life was turned around. Lubov found a new job as a governess for a wealthy family. She makes good money, and they trust and respect her. She has been working for this family for two years now.

Ruslan is busy building a house for his family. God also healed their son. He was prescribed glasses, but the whole family prayed and God miraculously restored the boy's eyesight!

During the few years Jesus walked the earth, we see the sunset of the law and the dawning of a new kind of man!

Jesus provoked wonder among His followers and criticism among His enemies during this season of transition. Everybody was asking, in effect, "What is happening now?"

- *"The disciples were amazed. 'Who is this man?' they asked. 'Even the winds and waves obey him!'"*[86]

- His critics said, *"'What is he saying? This is blasphemy! Only God can forgive sins!'"*[87]

---

[86] Matt. 8:27 NLT
[87] Mark 2:7 NLT

- His followers were shocked when they saw evil spirits respond to them. They said, *"Lord, even the demons obey us when we use your name!"*[88]

When we remove the wonder from Scripture and make it all mathematical equations or logical apologetics, we miss the wonder of who we are. There is an awe-struck wonder that springs from the thought of God coming to earth as a baby in a manger. There is a sense of inconceivable wonder that surrounds the concept of the Trinity. There is an incomprehensible wonder that comes from realizing that 2,000 years ago a man died on a cross as our substitute, paying for all we have ever done wrong!

There is much more to wonder at, but maybe the least appreciated truth is who God says *we* are. King David could not wrap his thoughts around it. He said, *"What are mere mortals that you should think about them, human beings that you should care for them? Yet you made them only a little lower than God and crowned them with glory and honor. You gave them charge of everything you made, putting all things under their authority."*[89]

The Apostle John raised the standard: *"Dear friends, we are already God's children, but he has not yet shown us what we will be like when Christ appears. But we do know that we will be like him, for we will see him as he really is."*[90] Allow the Christ in you to appear by allowing Him to appear through you to others.

---

[88] Luke 10:17 NLT
[89] Ps. 8:4–6 NLT
[90] 1 John 3:2–3 NLT

Does Not a King Live in You?

It's amazing that when religious leaders accused Jesus of acting like God, His logical response was to quote from Psalm 82, which says that humans are gods and sons of God.

"Rescue the poor and needy:

Deliver them out of the hand of the wicked.

They know not, neither do they understand;

They walk to and fro in darkness:

All the foundations of the earth are shaken.

I said, Ye are gods,

And all of you sons of the Most High.

Nevertheless ye shall die like men,

And fall like one of the princes." (Psalm 82: 4-7, ASV)

To experience God, we must allow Him to come down from the distant heavens and walk among us in flesh. We must allow Him to use our flesh.

The choice is ours. If we do not embrace this noble view of ourselves, we are doomed to live out our lives seeing ourselves as helpless, weak, and subject to circumstances. When an angel appeared to Gideon, he said, *"The Lord is with you, mighty man of valor"* (Judges 6:12). Gideon was hiding from his enemies at that time and did not feel any presence of God, nor did he have any strength or valor. God looked beyond Gideon's view of himself to what the Lord Himself thought of Gideon. The Lord said *"Go, I have sent you."* (Judges 6:14) That's all Gideon needed to know for victory. That's all we need to know for victory. When we know, then we go, and we will show that God is with us. Things have not changed much.

Can Jesus be the same in His Word as He was in His flesh?

Our answer to the question above must be *yes!* When we can see Him in His Word, we can expect to be like Him on earth today!

A real key to walking in our highest privilege and potential is to identify with what Scripture says about us, to the same extent that Jesus identified with what Scripture said about Him.

We get a glimpse of the secret of Jesus' power when we read His conversation with the two disciples as they walked along the road to Emmaus: *"Then he started at the beginning, with the Books of Moses, and went on through all the Prophets, pointing out everything in the Scriptures that referred to him."*[91]

Now that Jesus lives in our body, can we say the same things about ourselves? Can we think this way? Jesus said, *"I am the door."* Can we now say we are the door? Is He using us as a door for people to hear, respond to, and walk through out of darkness into light? He was the Healer. Now we are healers. He was the Savior. Now we are saving people. He was delivering. Now we are deliverers. He was giving peace. Now we are peace makers. Jesus said, *"I am*

---

[91] Luke 24:27 Message

129

the way." (John 14:6) We see amazing results as we speak to people who had been walking in a dead, empty way for thousands of years. They turn to the new way after hearing us speak of the life that Jesus is giving. We introduce a new way for them. When the leper cried out to Jesus for healing, Jesus did not ignore him. He touched him. When the lame man cried out to Peter and John, they did not turn from him but said, *"Such as I have I give to you." (Acts 3:6)* They then lifted him. We do not hide from the pain, suffering, and lack of humanity. Because Jesus now has His headquarters in our body, we become the answer to the world.

I imagine that as Jesus was growing up, He began to see Himself more and more in the ancient writings. As we grow in the Lord, do we experience the same identification with Scripture?

Are we as cognizant of what God says about us as we are of what God says about Jesus? The more we see ourselves in the Word, the more we will act like Him.

The religious leaders could not explain the boldness and power they saw in two common, uneducated fishermen named John and Peter, except that they had been with Jesus. They had been with Him and they were acting like Him. They must have identified with, embraced, and exhibited His character traits.

The key is seeing Jesus. As we see Him, we take on His likeness. When I think about bringing out all of our possibilities, I think of words like *"resemblance"* and *"copy,"* with similar words like "duplicate," "blueprint," "model," "prototype," "pattern," and "example."

Plenty of institutions have their theology all set up for you to sample. Their doctrines and dogma will satisfy every one of

130

your religious taste buds. But I believe there is something else for you, and that is why you are reading this book.

There is something that will take you beyond religion to the miracle life, beyond ritual to experience, beyond tradition to fresh thinking. It is when you decide to go beyond the borders that religion has politely erected that you will experience the unexplainable and truly see Jesus!

In several of our worldwide campaigns, Jesus has appeared to people. Usually, the people Jesus reveals Himself to are trapped in desperate conditions or cultural religion. A woman who had attended one of our meetings in Argentina said she saw Jesus come out of a ball of fire and say, "I do not reject you." She had rejected herself because of a divorce and was living in that sense of rejection.

On another occasion, in the city of Ufa in the Republic of Bashkortostan, an old Muslim grandmother was at the point of desperation because her alcoholic husband could not work and her son was in prison on drug charges. She was willing to walk into our tent for any kind of help. She sat down on the left side in the third row.

The meeting had just begun, and I was preaching that night. When she looked up, Jesus appeared on the stage, then came down to her, took her hand in His, and said, "I'm the One you have been looking for." Then He disappeared. After this, she came to the platform awe-struck, with tear-filled eyes. In a state of amazement she kept asking, "Is it really Him—Jesus?"

On several other occasions Jesus has made Himself personally known to people in a special way. But He always makes Himself known to all who will embrace Him as the Word of God. When we do that, we will see Him daily in

Scripture and hear Him calling to us to follow in the great adventure of life with Him!

Jesus said to His followers, *"Follow me, and I will make you fishers of men."*[92]

The Roman Empire was so afraid of this new authority that they tried to kill all Christians. However, these young believers would not cower under the boot of Caesar. A new fearlessness had entered into humankind that made the powers of this earth shake!

This same Spirit lives today in a new breed of men and women who are freeing themselves from the shackles of fear. They are committing to carry Good News to their republics without money, education, or government support. They are the next generation of God's communicators on the earth!

The Apostle Paul said our destiny is to be like Jesus: *"For whom he did foreknow, he also did predestinate to be conformed to the image of his Son, that he might be the firstborn among many brethren."*[93]

Paul had an interesting view of himself. He thought of himself as a man who had died and awakened to a second chance at life. He considered himself a dead man, yet still breathing. Dead men do not get offended at other men. Dead men do not scream back when they are screamed at. Dead men can be poked, kicked, mocked, and spit upon, and they still do not respond. The devil and his followers have no weapons when Christians do not respond in fear to their evil threats and actions.

---

[92] Matt. 4:19
[93] Rom. 8:29

This is the supremacy of love. It is a new kind of love that goes beyond human reaction to the reality of who we are.

Paul wrote, *"I am crucified with Christ: nevertheless I live; yet not I, but Christ liveth in me: and the life which I now live in the flesh I live by the faith of the Son of God, who loved me, and gave himself for me."*[94]

Paul reminded us to put on this new man. That means that as Christians we may not feel any more holy, smart, merciful, or powerful than we did before we accepted Jesus. But God's Word says we are new people, and we are to act like that is true! Paul put it this way: *"And have put on the new man, which is renewed in knowledge after the image of him that created him."*[95]

If we were separated from Jesus by an intercessor, priest, temple, sacrifice, religious membership, or something else, then we could consider this way of thinking of ourselves as extreme and unorthodox. But we are not separated from Jesus. God has chosen to live in us. Nothing separates us from our Creator![96]

Our bodies are called the temples of God. They were made holy when they were redeemed by the blood of Christ. They were made alive with the breath of God in the same way that Adam's body was made alive. Even when we were dead in trespasses, He made us alive together with Christ, and by grace we have been saved![97]

---

[94] Gal. 2:20
[95] Col. 3:10
[96] Rom. 8:38–39
[97] Eph. 2:5

Jesus' resurrection is a marvelous wonder. In the same breath with which God raised Jesus, He also raised us. We, like Christ, have been raised from the dead—raised to miracle life! We have the same life that Jesus has, it is not a different type or lesser quality of life. Therefore, we can be confident that we can boldly walk as He walked! Dare we believe this is possible? Yes! It is not beyond our potential when we see that we represent Him!

The story of scripture is a story of rediscovering yourself.

Our identity is always under attack. Satan attacked Adam and said if you eat this apple you will be like God. Adam was already in God's likeness, but did not see himself correctly.

When Satan came to Jesus to attack His identity, Satan received a different response. Satan said, *"If you be the Son of God."* (Matthew 4:6) Jesus' response was, *"It is written."* (Matthew 4:7) When we know what is written, we remove the question mark from our life.

Every time you pray and do not get an answer, your identification is under attack. Every time you give and do not receive, your identification is under attack.

I AM NOT ANNOINTED TO CONTROL THE WORLD.

I AM ANNOINTED TO CONTROL MY MIND.

Over 60 Nations

For over 30 years Drs. Kevin and Leslie
McNulty have penetrated over 60 nations
with the Gospel of Jesus Christ, face to
face before millions of people.

Guntur, India

Ponce, Puerto Rico

Benin, Cotonou

Chaco, Argentina

Tokyo, Japan

Paris, France

What is the Importance of Mass Evangelism?

1. It gives opportunity for a nation to hear good news without walls or religious barriers.
2. "It is the only way to keep up with the birth rate of a world where one-on-one evangelism may easily break down over time." – Louis Palau
3. It is a special moment for mass faith to be released and the impossible to happen.
4. It gives value to miracles that cause all men to believe in Jesus. John 11:47-48 "Then the chief priests and the Pharisees called a meeting of the Sanhedrin. "What are we accomplishing?" they asked. "Here is this man performing many signs. 48 If we let him go on like this, everyone will believe in him...""

Abidjan, Ivory Coast

Bangkok, Thailand

Gabon, West Africa

Leslie, Kevin and T. L. Osborn, Tokyo, Japan

T. L. Osborn and Kevin in San Jose, Costa Rica

OSBORN
Ministries, Int'l

November 8, 2007

918.743.6231 · Fax 918.749.0339
OSFO@aol.com · www.Osborn.org

TO THE PASTORAL COMMITTEE
(Miracle-Life Seminar & Crusade)

"We Christians are mirrors that brightly reflect the glory of the Lord. And as the Spirit of the Lord works within us, we become more and more like Him." 2Cor.3:18 LB

Drs. Kevin and Leslie are a remarkable couple with 30 years of miracle ministry in many nations, with great crowds. They are seasoned in miracle evangelism, and are talented in ministering to crowds of people. They have directed my *National Miracle Seminars* and *Public Festivals* for several years in many nations and every event has been triumphant. They are involved globally so take advantage of their schedule and welcome them to carry on just as you had planned for your area.

McNultys are mature faith ministers with years of successful evangelism and missions throughout the Far East, South America, all across Russia, Eurasia, Africa and Europe. They have worked with me in these great events for over 10 years and their record of ministry has been superb in all aspects.

They have initiated an awesome evangelism ministry across Russia and Eurasia, projecting 100 Gospel tents and Gospel Teams of young national preachers. Over 25 teams and tents are already in action. Thousands of young people are being saved in these ex-Soviet nations. They are installing a tent factory to fabricate their own tents and save costs in freight and customs.

I hope you will not miss this opportunity to welcome them to carry on the seminar and crusade just as if I had come.

The anointing that has rested on our events like the pillar of fire over Israel, can be like a fresh impartation to the ministers and believers of your area. They will see that God's miracle power is not limited to those who are better known, but only to those who have the faith to preach and to act on His Word—to those who love people enough to bring them His message.

I am deeply grateful to the McNultys for being such a significant part of ministering with me for several years. Our relationship has truly been confirmed by the hand of God.

Your special friend and co-worker with Christ,

T.L. Osborn
OSBORN Ministries Int'l

Dr. Kevin and Leslie and
T.L. Osborn in Ukraine

Drs. Leslie, Kevin and
Dr. T. L. Osborn in Benin

Dr. Kevin and Dr. T. L. Osborn
in Tokyo, Japan

PRESIDENTS

1Timothy 2:1-2 "First of all, then, I exhort that supplications, prayers, intercessions, and giving of thanks be made for all men, for kings and all who are in authority, so that we may lead a quiet and peaceable life in all godliness and reverence."

Kevin with President Laurent Gbagbo Ivory Coast

Kevin and Leslie with President Abel Pacheco Costa Rica

Kevin with President John Kuffuor Ghana, West Africa

Kevin with President Faure Essozimna Gnassingbé Togo, Africa

Kevin and Leslie with President Denis Sassou Nguesso, Brazzaville, Congo

Kevin with President Antoine Idji Kolawolé Benin, Cotonou

Kevin with President Omar Bongo Ondimba Gabon, West Africa

WORLDWIDE CONFERENCES

Paris, France
An amazing overflow conference at the national congress hall of Montreal, Paris, France.

Accra, Ghana, West Africa

Guatemala City, Guatemala

Santa Fe, Argentina
The national magazine UNO gave a two page full report on miracles.

Tokyo, Japan
*has never had 21 successive Gospel meetings in
its modern history.*

Oslo, Norway

Karaganda, Kazakhstan

MIRACLES

Salta, Argentina

A 4 year old boy with deformed and frozen ankles stands on his feet and takes his first steps for the first time!

Khon Kaen, Thailand

This woman had been blind for 6 months, but now she can see!

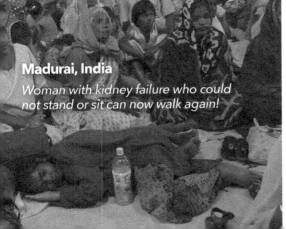

Madurai, India

Woman with kidney failure who could not stand or sit can now walk again!

Gabon

This young boy was blind since birth now demonstrates the miracle of sight!

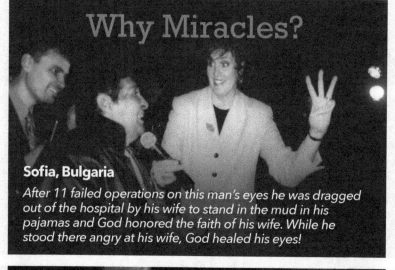

Why Miracles?

Sofia, Bulgaria

After 11 failed operations on this man's eyes he was dragged out of the hospital by his wife to stand in the mud in his pajamas and God honored the faith of his wife. While he stood there angry at his wife, God healed his eyes!

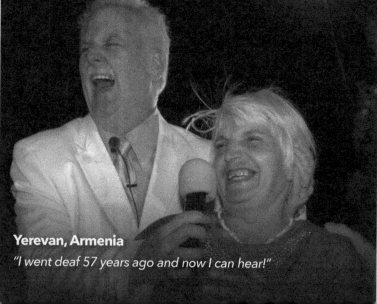

Yerevan, Armenia

"I went deaf 57 years ago and now I can hear!"

BOOKS

The 12th Chair

Born to Be Happy
(Russian Cover)

High Adventures
(Russian Cover)

Live Your Dream

Pathway to Healing

Pathway to Healing
(Russian Cover)

River & Rain
(French Cover)

You Can Do It,
Guntur, India

River & Rain

BOOKS

**High Adventures
in Christian Living**

Leslie McNulty book
(Russian Cover)

**In-Time Ideas for
Increase**
(Russian Cover)

Golden Nuggets
(Russian Cover)

McNulty book
(Russian Cover)

**Strength for Life
Mini-book**
(Russian Cover)

GIFT BOOKS

THOUSANDS OF BOOKS

Thousands of books given to the people of Gabon, Ghana, Benin, Togo, Japan, India, Costa Rica, Argentina, Ivory, Coast, Russia, Bulgaria.

HUNGRY FOR BOOKS
ACROSS COSTA RICA

What is the PURPOSE of books?
Books never change their message
Books never stop speaking
24 hours a day.
Books never get tired of
speaking their message.
Books go places we can't go.

100 TENTS

One hundred tents and teams across the 100 Nations, Republics, and Oblasts of Eurasia (former Soviet Union.

Bishkek, Kyrgystan

Chernovtsy, Ukraine

Ulan Bator, Mongolia

Tent evangelist training in Moscow, Russia

Ufa, Bashkortostan

Karaganda, Kazakhstan

Izhevsk, Russia

Tallinn, Estonia

Sofia, Bulgaria

Yaroslavl, Russia

The First Tent, Mozyr, Belarus

Yerevan, Armenia

EQUIPPING

Equipping and Empowering Future Tent Ministers and Teams

Moscow Training Center

Camp Meeting, Central Russia

Evangelists Conference, Moscow

Moscow Missions School

Nizhny Tagil, Ural Mountains school

FRIENDS OF THE MINISTRY

Charisma Magazine

ICFM March 2001

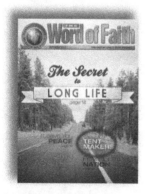

RHEMA Bible Training
Center

Kevin & TL Osborn on TBN

Daystar

Super Channel

Kenneth Copeland Ministries

Empowering Women Through Conferences Around the World

Leslie McNulty

Women's National Conference, Madurai, India

Women's National Conference, San Jose, Costa Rica

Women's National Conference, Karaganda, Kazakhstan

Women's Conference, Tokyo, Japan

Women's National Conference Accra, Ghana, Africa

Women's National Conference, Tallinn, Estonia

Women's National Conference, Libreville, Gabon, Africa

MULTI-MEDIA MINISTRY

USA Studio

Kevin & Leslie in USA studio

Praying over prayer requests in Russian Studio

LeslieMcNulty.com

Interviewing Dr. Jean LaCour, President of Net Institute

MIRACLES IN AMERICA

Apopka, Florida

"The doctor stated I have an incurable mass on my pancreas. When I went back the mass was gone!"

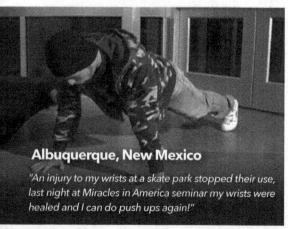

Albuquerque, New Mexico

"An injury to my wrists at a skate park stopped their use, last night at Miracles in America seminar my wrists were healed and I can do push ups again!"

Apopka, Florida

"I had arthritis and could barely walk for 34 years. On the first night God touched me. I went home and walked my dog and even ran!"

MIRACLES ABOUND ACROSS THE WORLD

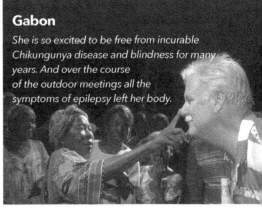

Gabon

She is so excited to be free from incurable Chikungunya disease and blindness for many years. And over the course of the outdoor meetings all the symptoms of epilepsy left her body.

Bulgaria

The Gypsy clan brings a child who was born deaf and mute to the meeting. In front of 40 gypsies he is completely healed, and his first word is "Hallelujah!"

Puerto Rico

This woman, 24 hours from amputation of her leg, receives her miracle with unspeakable joy and praise.

Gabon, Africa

Hunchbacked man for last 5 years receives a miracle when his pastor takes him to this meeting.

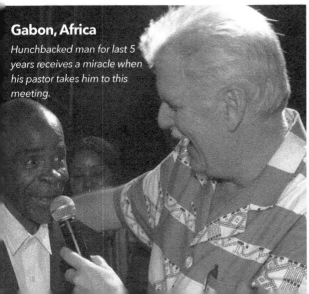

Armenia

This doctor came all the way from America. At age 3 he was thrown from a car and lost the hearing in his left ear. Tonight his hearing is restored!

HUMANITARIAN AID

Delivery of tents, generators, and food to Eurasia

Feeding the poor in Estonia

Truck loads of supplies for Eurasia

FIVE LOAVES & TWO FISHES

We have a goal of feeding and educating 12,000 children through the 5 Loaves and 2 Fishes program in India.

UKRAINE/EUROPE INITIATIVE

In partnership with World Harvest, Russia
And New Generation, Ukraine

Thank you for acting in the needy fields of the former Soviet Union and Europe.

We are on the move in these once spiritual nations to bring them the Good News by expanding the success we are experiencing in the Gospel Tent Ministry.

We are investing in factories, equipment, tents and teams to make it happen.

Every generation needs a power-filled witness of the living Jesus. Hundreds of young men and women and dozens of teams are ready to move on to the next city.

Respond through the sites listed below.

Get connected today!

Go to McNultyMinistries.com/give/

What can we do to help you grow in resource for these great movements? Receive the River and Rain" book written by Dr. Kevin McNulty NOW with a donation of $10.00 or more.

INDIA/ASIA MEDIA INITIATIVE

We are expecting the SALVATION OF INDIA and ASIA. By modern-era media technology, we are able to reach all 29 States of the crowded nation of India where one in every six people on the earth live.

We are creating self-sustaining mass media through social media, the internet and on TV News and Entertainment Channels. Have you considered that one broadcast television program sponsored by your family could change a family and even a whole community!

Income generated within the nation supports humanitarian efforts like our "5 Loaves and 2 Fish" Program by providing food, after school education and Bible knowledge to hundreds of villages.

You can make a difference in the nation's future.

Look below to see how you personally can be involved in transforming India and Asia.

Keep your eyes open for the upcoming release of Kevin's 2nd book in this series called "Unlimited Inspiration." It will fill you with a thousand reasons to stay inspired.

Remove poverty in India. Educate and feed a child for $15 a month.

Donate Now; go to
McNultyMinistries.com/Give

Watch recent Divinely Inspired Ideas for Life episodes at
LeslieMcNulty.tv

What must we do?

Allow our thoughts to ponder the new person we have become in Christ. You will never outperform the picture you have of yourself; you will always act like the person you think you are. We are told by Solomon that *"as a man thinks in his heart so is he."* (Proverbs 23:7) The fashion in which you see yourself decides what you will pursue. People will absorb their identity from family, neighborhood, culture, genetics, friends, or environment. The person who is born again absorbs his or her new identity from the revealed Word in his walk with Christ, and the examples he or she embrace in life.

People talk about having a second chance in life. Old people reflect on what could have been if they had made a different decision. The Good News is that everybody gets a second chance when God's life comes into them! They get a new destiny and a new road map with a great future. Embrace God's view of you and replace your old view.

He will not force His will on you. There are multiplied Biblical examples of God's plan for people, but their view of themselves is stopping it from happening. For example, when the 12 spies came back from the Promised Land, they did not speak against God or the great land He said was theirs. Ten of the spies just could not think of themselves as winning in a battle with the giants because they saw themselves as grasshoppers. They criticized themselves. God was for them, but they were against themselves. You are only able to do what you see yourself doing.

You have to see what God sees, to feel what God feels. Christians believe in the greatness of God, but they see no greatness in themselves. It might surprise you, but a sinner who feels good about himself will produce more than a

167

Christian who does not feel good about himself!

You can start building that self-image today. It will be more important to you than a Harvard college education or a major position in the top 500 companies of the world. When God called you, He put a picture of yourself within you.

Imprint that image into yourself often. Speak that picture to yourself. Encircle that idea with your faith. Faith is voice activated so start talking about it. Feed it. What you feed will grow. What you starve will diminish.

We have been given a marvelous foundation from which to build a life. When we see the mindless destruction, death, and abuse that so many people face across the world, I am so thankful for understanding the root that my tree springs from. It is wonderful not to be tied up in confusing traditions, mysterious cultural worship, or modern mind gymnastics. The root of redemption brings finality to constant practices that work your way to heaven. Redemption identifies the real issue of man's sinful nature and its removal by one who had no sin. It gives the world a second chance if they choose to believe it, and closes the book on laws that could not fulfill God's standard anyway.

It is a breath of fresh air to understand that the whole world revolves around two men: the first Adam and the last Adam. The first Adam got us into the mess of a hopeless, fallen state, separated from our Creator. The last Adam, who is Jesus, became the final solution, Who more than restored our relationship with our unseen Father.

12"Therefore, as through one man sin entered into the world, and death through sin; and so death passed unto all men, for that all sinned . . . 15 But not as the trespass, so also [is] the free gift. For if by the trespass of the one the many died, much more did the grace of God, and the gift by the grace of the one man, Jesus Christ, abound unto the many. 16 And not as through one that sinned, [so] is the gift: for the judgment [came] of one unto condemnation, but the free gift [came] of many trespasses unto justification. 17 For if, by the trespass of the one, death reigned through the one; much more shall they that receive the abundance of grace and of the gift of righteousness reign in life through the one, [even] Jesus Christ." (Romans 5:12, 15-17, American Standard Version)

Stay up by feeding on the realities of your new life in Christ, while you diet the critical crisis that this world revolves in.

Evaluate the relationships you are in. What you keep hearing is eventually what you will believe. You will perform to the level that you are persuaded is your level. I started a ministry with a program called "Each One Reach One." At that time, I could not see beyond one person. Time, meditation, experience and exposure grew my abilities to speak to multitudes.

Get a picture of what you want to be, and start living in that picture. In my early days, I would spend hours at the local city airport just picturing myself flying. Every extra dime I made I put into plane tickets to fly to a new destination and challenge myself to grow. Your posture mirrors your self-portrait. How you act reveals who you are becoming. He planned a great future for you, but the plans and purposes God has for you cannot override the plans you see yourself doing.

How do you know when you are changing? Your self-depiction decides how you will be treated. In my travels with a senior spokesmen for Christianity I closely observed what he would allow, and what he would not allow. How we posture ourselves is not based on other's approval or disapproval. It was a priceless discovery and the key to determining where ministry would be received, as well as what nations would be ready for revival.

The drawing you have embraced of yourself determines how you will be treated. Many women in abusive relationships with their husbands came out of an abusive relationship with their father or family. The picture you see of yourself will determine how long others can torment you.

God has put a great value on you, and has demonstrated that worth by substituting His only begotten Son to take your place at a cross where sin, sickness, and all the fallen curse of mankind was emptied on Him.

That is the Father's vote for you. Your picture of yourself determines the value you put on yourself and what you will allow into your life. When Satan tries to destroy you, he goes after the picture you have of yourself. Do not paint your picture in watercolors, but in stone. Engrave that image of what redemption has portrayed you to be, so Satan will have to say, "Jesus I know, and Paul I know, and you I know." Satan knows that a confused self-image will be a doorway to sin, and sin's greatest damage is the loss of belief in ourselves. The greatest loss that sin produces in our lives is the loss of the self-portrait we have. We turn from the light and see the shadows of weakness and failure. The only solution is to turn around and look into the light, for no darkness is present there. Remind yourself that you will never outperform the picture you have of yourself, and you will always act like the person you think you are. Keep this idea before you often until new habits that lift you up are established.

Like my mentor before me, when I walk out the airplane door and onto the tarmac to face a crowd of people who have been waiting, planning, and expecting good things from my visit, I recognize that I am the embodiment of hope for that nation.

I am not concerned about how many witch doctors have planned to put curses on me. I am not concerned about how many news articles the religious hierarchy may have purchased to give negative press to our coming. Rather, I posture my thoughts to be a blessing. I consider all that God would like a human being to be and have and do!

I consider the great prophecies that have gone before us concerning the day that we live in. I consider the great promises that Jesus has made concerning those who go in His name. I consider the great need of hurting humanity, and the Good News that God has paid the price to meet that need.

These are the things that inspire me as I consider traveling thousands of miles to stand in front of the lost, sick, poverty-stricken, and fearful people of a nation. The living church is the cure for the world's ills, and the world is the reason for the church's existence.

171

As you walk out onto the stage of life,
hold your head high and be the voice
of God to your hurting world.

Pick well who you allow to put a value on you!

CHAPTER 4

HEAVEN'S CHAIR

Do we have Heaven's perspective? Can we go beyond what we see?

Are words helping or hurting us?

Can Jesus be the same in your body in the 21st Century as He was in a body of a Jew in the 1st century?

Jesus Gives a Different Perspective.

COMMUNISM says: "You must serve the state for your value."

CAPITALISM says: "Your value is based on what you can produce. Without employment you are worthless."

POVERTY says: "You are inferior and a second-class citizen."

FAME says: "You're a nobody until your name is in lights."

RELIGION says: "God is so high, you must be low. God is so smart, you must be ignorant. God is so holy, you must be a sinner."

JESUS says:

> *"I have come that you might have life and that life with complete fullness."*

(John 10:10 Good News Translation)

> *"As the Father has sent me, I send you."*

(John 17:18)

> *"You are the light of the world. You are the salt of the earth."*

(Matt. 5:13-14)

Scripture gives us more than a glimpse of the position we have in heaven while we live on earth. The sacred text presents the ultimate transforming ideas: God is portrayed, and man is pictured as made in His image. This seems impossible for the unredeemed to accept, because it provides such a lofty position for every man, woman, and child who identifies with Jesus Christ.

Paul said he identified completely with Christ in His death, but also in His resurrection and in His place seated in heaven. To be seated in Christ is to take a chair in a high position. There you find your place of rest. When you see yourself seated in this chair, you get a new perspective on your earthly problems. They seem very small. This is a place of great vision, joy, and authority. Our prayers are pointed downward toward the mountains on earth below us. We are no longer looking upward for help! A change of perspective can give a change of result.

There are moments in ministry when we must address the situation about our God, and not use up time to address God about the situation.

Kevin lifts the nation in Gabon, West Africa

A terrible storm blew in on the fourth night of open-air ministry in Gabon. I heard the report and saw the dangerous clouds, but I did not cancel the event that 60,000 people would soon be attending. Faith stirred deep in my soul as I spoke to the black clouds to split; then I got into the car and headed out to preach. It was a moment to remember when the clouds started to form a circle with a giant hole where the grounds were. It was a moving night of ministry and healing for the nation.

This was a time to get above the clouds with a voice ringing from heaven for the souls of mankind!

There are times when prayer is sweet communion with the Father and Jesus. There are other times when we must bind and loose things on this earth. God is expecting *us* to address the mountain, not address Him about the mountain. We were facing a closure of the border between Belarus and Ukraine for five days during a critical opening of the Ukraine for Tent Ministry. The drivers were so frustrated that they threatened to leave our tents on the border and go home. Thousands of dollars and thousands of lives were at stake. It was time to address the situation and the spirits behind it with an unrelenting fervency. We were standing in the field in Crimea with one hundred volunteers calling on the border to loose our tents and let us in. Gala, from our Eurasian team, saw a vision of the border cross bar rising. Within minutes we got a phone call letting us know that the trucks got through!

Tents arrive in Crimea

Does God the Father sit alone in Heaven?

The truth is, He is not alone at all. Not only is there a heavenly host of angels, but there is also a great crowd of saints. However, one invited guest rarely enjoys the festivities or fellowship of heaven. Do you know who that invited guest is? It is you!

Scripture tells us that we are seated together in heavenly places in Christ Jesus.[98] You might think this is for the future—that someday your physical body will be there. But this is also a present reality. Understanding it will help you greatly as you navigate the tribulations on this earth.

Our position in Christ is secure. It is when we look at ourselves from *His* perspective that we rise above the mountains and enemies before us. Jesus is waiting for us to put those obstacles beneath our feet. The Bible tells me that He prepares a table before me in the presence of my enemies.[99] He is calling you and me to sit at that table now to enjoy what He has put on it for us.

We need to get comfortable in our heavenly chair, seated with Christ, so we can be comfortable in our earthly chair in front of our enemies. How is that possible? As Jesus walked down the road one day with His disciples, He asked them who people said He was.[100] They replied that people were calling Him John the Baptist, or Elijah, or another one of the prophets risen from the dead. But when Jesus pressed them about *their* beliefs, Peter responded that He was the Christ, the Son of the living God. Jesus opened up a new world to Peter once He saw that Peter had this belief. The people gladly called Jesus a prophet, just as today people gladly call Him a teacher and a prophet.

Do people understand that His prophesies are about Himself?

He can only be God or a liar to say what He said of Himself being the only way to the Father. Peter said, *"You are the*

---

[98] Eph. 2:6
[99] Ps. 23:5
[100] Matt. 16:13

Lord." (Matthew 16:16) This is the title given only to God. When Caesar required all people to call Him Lord, exalted one, god among men, Christians would not because there is only one God worthy of the title Lord. So Caesar crucified the Christians for calling Jesus the Lord, Supreme One, worthy of all praise.

If you want to enjoy heaven's table of blessing, you must begin by accepting this revelation: that Jesus Christ was God on earth, God with man. Once Peter had this revelation, Jesus could talk differently to him. First, Jesus told Peter that flesh and blood had not revealed this to him; rather, the Father above had given him this revelation.[101]

Today we pride ourselves on how much knowledge we can accumulate. The amount of human knowledge used to double every few generations. Now it doubles every few years. In the midst of all that knowledge, we can lose the few truths that really transform us. These are not just information; they are truths that the Father reveals to us.

As soon as Peter got the revelation of who Jesus really was, Jesus gave Peter a revelation of who Peter was. Jesus changed his name from Simon to Peter so that Peter would see himself differently. Then Jesus began to reveal to Peter the new authority that he would have because of knowing who Jesus was. Jesus said He would give Peter the keys of heaven. Keys represent authority.

Whatever a believer binds on earth would be bound in heaven. Whatever a believer will loose on earth will be loosed in heaven.[102] Jesus invited Peter and all other believers to be seated in heaven's chair so they could exercise the author-

---

[101] Matt. 16:17
[102] Matt. 16:19

ity of that new position on earth. All believers were given the keys of heaven's authority because they were seated in heaven's chair.

Dear friend, you now sit in heavenly places in Christ Jesus with these same keys. Pull your chair up to the table and eat of the goodness of God on earth in the presence of your enemies!

God said of the person who would set his love upon Him, *"I will set him on high, because he hath known my name."*[103]

Jesus was our example of God on earth. One reason He came was to give us a model to follow. His Word is now our word. His attitudes are now our attitudes. His resources are now our resources. He has lifted us up spiritually to sit with Him in heavenly places. Even if our bodies are destroyed, we are not. Our focus on Him brings us to the place of highest privilege, honor, and action.

We enter into this chair of highest status by faith. Our senses tell us nothing of this noble position. Our natural eyes have not seen it, but our spiritual eyes allow us to see ourselves above the natural elements in God's finished work. Scripture tells us we are seated at the right hand of God in heaven because we are in Christ.

> *"You who sit down in the High God's presence, spend the night in Shaddai's shadow, say this: 'God, you're my refuge. I trust in you and I'm safe!'"*[104]

> *"Then he picked us up and set us down in highest heaven in company with Jesus, our Messiah."*[105]

---

[103] Ps. 91:14 ASV
[104] Ps. 91:1–2 Message
[105] Eph. 2:6 Message

This seat gives us a commanding prayer position. Seeing ourselves lifted up to this lofty place challenges us. Our posture should be one of looking down on our situation from a place of abundant supply. Now that we have been lifted above circumstances and seated in authority, our position in prayer allows us to deal with the problems.

With one of the national evangelistic conferences about to begin in Moscow, we had done all the natural preparation possible. Invitations were sent out and food was evaluated for the guests. The cost of travel, housing and books was all budgeted. It was the morning of departure and still no income had come in to provide for this major event. We checked our hearts and called the money to come with conviction of the scripture and rightness of the cause. We then decided to go to the airport. As we walked to the car, I received an amazing phone call from a partner that $10,000 was on the way. What a victory and a relief! The Lord had dealt with him weeks ago, but he had just remembered and wanted us to know he was sending it immediately. There is a prayer that is spoken with the voice of heaven, and it is well to find that voice.

Traditional prayers go upward, looking for heavenly attention. Now our prayers are directed downward from our chair in heaven. From this high position we speak to the conditions we face on earth. Our chair in heaven gives us perfect association with God. He accepts us and identifies us as His own.

Our chair in heaven provides us with perfect access to the throne of God. He is not hiding His love or His presence from us. Our chair gives us perfect authority. We sit in Christ, who has been given all authority in heaven and on earth.[106] He is waiting for us to make His enemies His footstool.[107]

Our feelings, thoughts, and experiences may not indicate that we have such a great position. But we must forget our present indicators and look through the eyes of faith! Faith sees Scripture, not our circumstances, as the final word. Faith sees what our natural eye cannot. Faith goes beyond the veil of the natural world to the one in which we will live forever.

The Scriptures tell us, *"God, being rich in kindness, because of His great love with which He loved us, even being dead in the trespasses, did make us to live together with the Christ, (by grace ye are having been saved,) and did raise us up together, and did seat us together in the heavenly places in Christ Jesus, that He might show, in the ages that are coming, the exceeding riches of His grace in kindness toward us in Christ Jesus."*[108]

Our seating together in heavenly places in Christ Jesus is a position of great esteem that we have through no effort of our own. Yet this position has not registered on the hearts of many Christians, because their eyes are on their present troubles and their thoughts are clouded with natural issues. But God is inviting us all to sit at the table He has prepared in the presence of our enemies. He is inviting us to sit in His light, not in the shadow of death.

---

[106] Matt. 28:18
[107] Heb. 10:12–13
[108] Eph. 2:4-7 YLT

We do not see things as they are.
We see things as we are!

Part 1

YOU CAN ONLY BE THE SELF YOU SEE

If you cannot see yourself lifted to Heaven's Chair, you will struggle with insignificance and a lack of power in an uncomfortable earthly chair. To live only for a position appointed to you by yourself or other people is to limit your life.

We speak a lot about vision because it is one of the major abilities that sets us apart from the rest of creation. Monkeys do not wake up wondering what they can become. Stars do not look for the next galaxy to shine in. Trees do not dream of a distant forest to grow in!

The sign of our God-like quality is our vision of a higher standard of living, excelling, integrity, achievement, and increase. To deny this quality of our humanity called vision is to lower ourselves in God's creative order from our lofty position as sons and daughters of the Creator Himself!

God has left us with a Book to capture our imaginations with His intentions and plans for us. His words echo through every generation, calling us to stand up in righteousness. To think otherwise is to live in a false humility that diminishes the human spirit. We do right because we are right. We were made right when Christ exchanged His righteousness for our sin. We now stand in harmony with the Creator, just as Jesus stood in harmony with Him.

God has a major problem. He has lots of ideas, but He needs people to act on those ideas.

God is great and powerful; however, He is limited. He has restrained Himself to act only though His body. His kingdom is within you, and He reigns from His kingdom. God requires flesh to accomplish His work.

He needed Jesus in the flesh to do His work. He needs *you* in your flesh to do His work. Jesus was God's Word made flesh.[109] God needs your voice to release His power through His Word!

A Profound Mystery

There is a profound mystery here that is almost unexplainable. After several years in the desert spending time re-examining the scripture that he had memorized, the Apostle Paul stated the very heart of the Gospel when he said that this mystery of the Gospel is *"Christ in you, the hope of glory."*[110]

Paul said about himself words that we need to say about ourselves, words that will affect our self-image. He said, *"I am crucified with Christ: nevertheless I live; yet not I, but Christ liveth in me."*[111]

Paul totally identified with Jesus Christ and stood one with Him in purpose, power, and image. Now we can totally identify with Christ in honor and privilege as Paul did.

Here is God's great offer: "You give Me your body, I will give you My Spirit, and we will have a Christian!"

Christ's eternal life and our mortal life are vying daily for our attention. Often it takes a radical wake-up call to remind us that earth is not our final destination, and only a fraction of our time is spent here!

[109] John 1:14
[110] Col. 1:27
[111] Gal. 2:20

I have a friend who accidentally experienced death while repairing a bus. His skull was fractured when a brake spun off at high speed and hit him. His body lay in a pool of blood; yet he said his spirit began to rise and hover over the bus.

In this elevated state he saw his wife get out of the bus and bend down over his limp body. Then, with a piercing voice of authority that shook heaven, she commanded him to come back into that body. He had two children to rear, so she spoke as a woman who would not take no for an answer!

My friend said that instead of going up into heaven, he came back down into his broken body. He told me the greatest revelation he received while separated from his body was that he was helpless to help himself when he did not have a body.

He must have felt as God the Father feels. God is spirit. What does He want? He wants a body. He wants to have an influence on the affairs of mankind.

Our bodies give us the right to exercise God's authority on the earth. God created the first man, Adam, out of the dust of the earth and breathed His life into him. Then He gave Adam the authority to rule the earth. Adam gave that authority to Satan. Jesus won this authority back through His sacrifice, and has returned it to mankind.

Jesus is resurrected and now lives in His new body. Jesus is a King, and His Kingdom is within you. He reigns through you. When God acts, it is through the Body of Christ on earth.

God can only go where your feet take Him. He can only touch the people you touch. He sees through your eyes

185

and speaks through your mouth. His words are all-powerful, but for that power to be released they must be spoken through lips of faith!

We are beginning to see the love connection between God the Father and His family. We need God, but He also needs us because He is spirit, and we are flesh. We need His Spirit to live. He needs our flesh to show the world His love. He makes a deal with us: He gives us His Spirit in return for our flesh. He identifies with us and we now identify with Him.

Man was created to be like God

Man was created to be like God—to be noble and have dominion on earth. Man was to take heaven's blueprint and establish it on earth as an example of what earth will look like in the future. Jesus said to pray that the kingdom come on earth as it is in heaven. We must conclude then that God's plan is that we be like Jesus.

Humanity was first made in the image of God. Genesis 1:27 says, *"So God created man in his own image, in the image of God created he him; male and female created he them."* Then God re-made man through Jesus' finished work on the cross. We can now walk in the resurrected life Jesus experienced when He rose from the tomb. Colossians 3:9–10 says, *"Ye have put off the old man with his deeds; and have put on the new man, which is renewed in knowledge after the image of Him that created him."* Unfortunately, religion turned our authority into an institution, and took the authoritative Word of God out of the language of the people. This act propelled the world into the Dark Ages. Why were they dark? The church had the scripture only in a dead language of Latin. The people were not allowed to read it and did not hear it in church, so the world went dark. When did the dark ages end? When Martin Luther put the Bible in the language of the common man, and the Gutenberg press published it for all. Today we can read for ourselves what God's original intention was, and why He had to send Jesus as a living example of His plan for us.

Our authority comes when we see ourselves as Jesus saw Himself: sent by the Father and representing His will on the earth in the flesh. Dare we think this highly of ourselves?

There is a blindness in the people who deny Jesus as Lord.[112] And there is a blindness in the Church about our position in Him to carry out what He began.

What Is Missing?

Have you ever walked out the door and asked yourself, "What am I missing?" You might have run a checklist in your mind of what you needed to carry with you to get yourself through the day: keys, wallet, phone, pen, glasses, etc. But have you considered that what really carries you through the day is your self-identity?

It is only your understanding of your own value, destiny, and self-worth that helps you overcome the many tricks of the devil, the flesh, and the world.

One of the fastest-growing crimes today is identity theft. People have lost their bank accounts and credit ratings. Often they suffer emotionally and financially for years when this theft occurs. But there is an identity that no one can steal from you because no human gave it to you. It is your new identity in Christ. Many times, because of tradition or unscriptural preaching, people have lost the sense of who they really are.

---

[112] 2 Cor. 4:4

Our identity in Christ was bought and paid for by the precious blood of Jesus on the cross 2,000 years ago when He sacrificed Himself as our substitute. Jesus did not just pardon us—He legally redeemed us so that no accusation of guilt or feeling of shame could control our lives. When Jesus hung on that cross, we hung with Him. Our problem was not just the devil, but our sin nature. We had to identify with Jesus in death to identify with Him in life. The devil can do nothing beyond death. The curse ends at death. Sickness ends at death. All torment and trouble end at death.

We died so we could live a new life beyond the power of Satan and this fallen world.

No one can put down a son or daughter of God unless that child of God chooses to think lowly of him or herself. Jesus said that if He is lifted up, He will draw all people unto Him. He is never a put-down. There is only one way to go when you are connected to Him, and that is up! That is, up in attitude, up in perspective, up in ability and up in self dignity.

A friend of ours who helped us launch our work in Russia was yelled at for 15 minutes by an airport bus driver. She was brought to tears as she walked down the center aisle of the bus, verbally abused and diminished.

We had to shake her and say, "Who is that man—that unbeliever who hates himself and hates his job? He is a victim of his society and has decided to victimize you with his words. Do not accept his words. He does not know what he says or who he speaks to!"

This was a revelation to her. She did not have to give people the right to make her a victim of their anger and insecurities. You do not have to absorb the label that other people, or your past, or your family, or even yourself, have put on you. God has marked you for a wonderful destiny!

Who can put down what God has lifted up?

Who can degrade what God has put great value on?

Who can insult whom God sings the praises of?

The redeemed are proud of God's finished work in them, but arrogance has no place in the believer. That is the fruit of low self-esteem crying out for recognition. All humans need to feel significant and that they really are special. Do not mistake pride for arrogance. We want our doctor to be proud of his work if we need an emergency operation. Who wants a doctor with only a 50% success rate? We want our stockbroker to be proud of his record in picking good stocks, who wants to hire a failing broker? We want our car mechanic to be proud of his work, because we do not want mistakes on a car we are driving 70 miles an hour! There is no place for arrogant Christians who are loud and brutish in actions, trying to hide the inferiority they feel. When we truly discover our value to our Creator, and our value as a unique human redeemed in Christ, then arrogance is replaced with healthy pride.

We will not belittle what God redeemed.

We will not put down what God raises up.

We will not think about ourselves contrary to how God thinks about us!

God has begun a significant work in all of us. Much of the world looks to its own efforts to find importance. Many people make their own gods. Some remote tribes consider alligators to be their ancestors. Many modern professors consider their predecessors to have been monkeys!

The goal of the Gospel is you. You are a new creation who is enlightened, entrusted, equipped, and energized to continue the work Jesus began two millenniums ago!

I am satisfied by study, revelation, and experience that God alone is my origin. I reflect Him. The saddest disease I encounter as I travel the world is the unease of those who are made by circumstance and other forces to feel small, needy, and helpless.

What could be holding people back from their new potential in Christ? Could it be that we look for our identity in our genetics?

You might say that you are just like your father or mother because of the genes you received, but your heavenly Father has given you a new set of molecules made whole in Christ. In this world of the blame game, you can claim your habit of destructive behavior or perverted acts as something you were born with. Okay, but what about the new birth? Isn't that stronger than the natural one? Doesn't that count? So many claim the ailments and diseases of their parents, but what of their new spiritual Father and His DNA now recreated in you?

Others gain a negative identity from constant thought patterns of failure, addiction, or depression. It is true that you are what you think, but a transformed life brings transformed thoughts! You might blame your unhappy lifestyle on thoughts that you have had all your life, calling yourself a loser. However, isn't the message of scripture to get new thoughts, a new spirit, new power, and a new start? To RE-PENT is to change your way of viewing your world.

Thoughts can be replaced so that a victim can become a victor. A hell-bound person in the most negative of situations can change into a person who has an eternity in heaven. If that cannot stimulate new thought, what can? Others say they are who they are because of the neighborhood they grew up in. It's great to have a beautiful and safe community, but some of the greatest men and women of the ages came from difficult places and people. It is choice and not environment that dictates our future. Friends and environment might be our excuse for our problems, depression, low self-esteem, and worthless feelings. You might be in the ghetto, but it's a choice whether you let the ghetto in you. God has put peace, power, and purpose in you. Find a garden where these qualities can grow, even in the worst neighborhood.

One of my mission trips took me to the deepest part of Siberia, Russia. While the ice still held its bitter grip on the streets, we conducted a conference to which everyone was welcome.

In the middle of my message, I noticed a small, timid man quietly sit down in the back row. (I later learned his name was Boris, from the city of Neryungry.) I felt impressed to say, "If you are a street cleaner, be a great street cleaner for God!"

Tears welled up in his eyes. When I spoke to him after the meeting, he told me he was a street cleaner. He also confessed that he had been on his way that morning to kill himself with the gun he still had in his possession.

But as he walked by the building where I was preaching, he overheard the strange sound of a foreigner. Filled with curiosity, he entered.

I spoke directly to his heart. Then Jesus spoke to him and said, "Boris, I love you. Go into the ministry and write a book."

Boris began to weep. He said, "Kevin, will you help me write a book?" I told him I must go on to the next city, but that I would pray for his new life and success.

Seven years later, as I held on to a railing on a train in Moscow's underground transit system on which nine million people travel each day, I turned and looked into the eyes of a man whose gaze was riveted on me.

Kevin with Boris from Neryungry in the Moscow metro.

"Boris, is that you?" I asked.

He leapt to his feet, hugged me, and cried, "It is! It is!"

"What are you doing here so far away from your hometown?" I asked.

He said he was finishing up his Bible school education and was on his way to pastor a church! Then he reminded me, "I am going to write that book!"

Recently I met him, and he now heads up a significant ministry to the Jews.

There is nothing like the power of a transformed life! It is a life that has found value, purpose, and a friend in Jesus. God offers a new image to all humanity, while breathing His life into all who will call upon the name of the Savior, Jesus!

People cannot rise above their image of themselves or act better than how they think of themselves. A leader or minister cannot reproduce *what he or she wants* in the lives of others—only *who* he or she *is.* That is why I consider living in the likeness of Christ as the first step to the miracle life.

This miracle life should be our standard—our yardstick and guide. Where can we find this standard? It cannot be just my opinion or the theological opinion of a denomination or church. Only the clear, written Word of God will stand the weight of confirming God's newborn children as rightful heirs of miraculous expectation. When we read what God says about us, and we agree with it by saying it about ourselves, all of hell and all of heaven take notice.

193

PART 2
USING YOUR WORD CONNECTION

Your image is locked into the words you say about yourself!

Most people do not recognize that the words they speak about themselves are the seeds they sow for their future. Paul made it clear that God cannot be mocked. Whatever a man sows he shall reap.[113]

Words are seeds, and seeds are energizers. Choose well what you want to energize in your life. If this is true, then where do energized words come from? Jesus said that out of the abundance of the heart a person speaks.

Words were not given to the human race to declare the way things are. They were given to declare the way things will be!

He also said that when we drink the water He gives, then out of us will flow a continuous refreshing flow of water to eternal life. That sounds very poetic, but it boils down to the source of your life being within you, and you decide what is put in you. It is not the government, family, culture, color or age that decides what you say and believe and see in your life. Let that which comes from you be life to others.

---

[113] Gal. 6:7

Jesus said the Word is the seed, and the soil is the heart.[114] Since God is never fooled, do not fool yourself regarding what you are saying and thinking about yourself. Recognize these powerful forces God has given you. Use them to your benefit, or ignore them to your undoing!

What is the seed that God gives humanity? It is the ideas He has inspired and recorded for history in the book we call the Bible. These ideas are what He has done for us and who He has made us. And they tell us what we can do now as a result of who we are. Armed with these ideas, we can form a new image of ourselves apart from our past, our present circumstances, and our self-imposed limitations for the future. This truth will free us from a victim mentality.

In the world of tennis, a game which I greatly enjoy, there is a basic rule that carries me through the emotional ups and downs of a match. More than once I have snatched victory from the hands of defeat by remembering this simple principle. It is the one thing I must do to win: *keep my eye on the ball!*

I am not fighting my opponent, the sun, the wind, the crowd, or myself. My opponent can distract me with movement, a verbal outburst, or delays, but he cannot change the ball.

In life you can experience changes in the economy, the people around you, the environment, and other circumstances. But one thing should not change: *keep your eye on where you are going!*

---

[114] Mark 4:3–20

Talk about where you are going. Think about where you are going. Feel strongly about where you are going. Believe in where you are going.

But what about the temporary score? What if you are behind? That does not change where you are going, so why think about it? The Apostle Paul gave us some things to think about. He said, *"Finally, brothers, whatever is true, whatever is honorable, whatever is just, whatever is pure, whatever is lovely, whatever is commendable, if there is any excellence, if there is anything worthy of praise, think about these things."*[115] In other words, do not let your mind go into the gutter of worry, fear, or anxiety about what might happen. In tennis, if you take your eye off the ball, you lose sight of the only thing you can control. If you allow yourself to be distracted, defeat is guaranteed. Today, make a quality decision to keep your eyes on what you want. Celebrate it. Pray about it. Think on it only. Jesus said that whatever you desire, when you pray, believe you receive it and you shall have it![116]

Today you can start sowing good words, thoughts, and faith for the person you want to be tomorrow. The Apostle Paul made it clear when he said that we do not receive what God sows or what others sow—we only receive what we sow or say about ourselves.[117] What the ancient text says is still true: *"Death and life are in the power of the tongue: and they that love it shall eat the fruit thereof."*[118] Our future is as far away as our tongue!

---

[115] Phil. 4:8 ESV
[116] Mark 11:24
[117] Gal. 6:7
[118] Prov. 18:21

We often hear testimonies of spectacular changes from people who have been in extreme emotional depression. People without hope for a long period of time often conclude that death is better than life and become suicidal. Many people do not choose to kill themselves dramatically with a gun, a knife, or poison; instead, they lead suicidal lifestyles through alcohol or drug abuse. Statistics worldwide show the number of these people are increasing every year. The first steps out of this lifestyle are for them to see and say what Scripture declares to be "the new you."

Kevin and Leslie's meetings in French Congo

In Brazzaville, the capital of the Republic of the Congo, we were ministering before a crowd of 60,000 people. Suddenly a torrential rain poured down and knocked out the sound system. At that moment all I could do was have the people sing, then I prayed for the sick.

197

One lady within the sound of my voice was preparing to commit suicide because of a terrible ringing in her ears and an infection in her head. She could barely hear the prayer I was shouting at the top of my voice over the pelting rain. But as the Word reached her ears, Jesus totally healed her. She saw herself wanting to live again. It is amazing that God reveals Himself to any who will hear His Word and act on it!

All who believe that Jesus Christ is Lord and Redeemer are in the Body of Christ. God has entrusted His plan for the world to His body. See your body as Christ's body practically functioning on earth. It is the noblest place of highest privilege for a human. When Jesus comes into you at the new birth, He brings His plan for the world with Him. You are enlarged and empowered to do the impossible, but only if you can see yourself doing it!

God needs His Word spoken on lips of faith to do His work. We do the possible—He does the impossible!

God's Word is the true source of an image of a righteous man or woman.[119] Slave owners in America in the early 1800's knew that people would not be slaves if they could read for themselves what God said about them, so they passed laws forbidding slaves to be taught to read and write. Learning to read was the first step toward grasping President Abraham Lincoln's Emancipation Proclamation. It was also the first step toward knowing God's proclamation of a new position in Christ! James 1:23–24 (NLT 1996) says, *"If you just listen and don't obey, it is like looking at your face in a mirror but doing nothing to improve your appearance. You see yourself, walk away, and forget what you look like."*

---

[119] 2 Cor. 3:17–18; James 1:23–25

God has always used words to work His will. In the beginning, the Bible says the world was created by words.[120] The kings and prophets of the Old Covenant received words that revealed who God was.

**Words are containers of life.
They project images.
These images are
the building blocks of the future!**

Jesus declared that when we receive the Holy Spirit, we become His witnesses and His Word-speakers to all creation.[121] Jesus said His words are Spirit and life![122]

I was raised in church. For 22 years I attended the services and heard the words, but no transforming personal experience ever happened. Then one day under a maple tree on the Michigan State University campus in the U.S.A., I spoke out of my heart and asked Jesus to come into my life.

Suddenly my spiritual eyes were opened! I felt the cleaning agent of the Holy Spirit, like a scrub brush, wash away my sin and remove my guilt. I saw my past as forgiven. Then I sensed heaven open up, and for the first time I knew I was going there. My hope was transformed into a knowing.

---

[120] Gen. 1:3
[121] Acts 1:8
[122] John 6:63

Everybody I knew growing up hoped they were going to heaven, but for the first time, I knew! It happened when my words and my heart hooked up with the truth that God wanted me to know.

Jesus said, *"And ye shall know the truth, and the truth shall make you free."*[123]

In ministry I have discovered that the Holy Spirit is always present when the Word is preached. He is present the same way He was when Jesus preached. It is the same with the power of God to heal the sick. It is always available, whether I feel strong or weak, healthy or sick, inspired or depressed.

Khon Kaen, Thailand

---

[123] John 8:32

At a meeting in Thailand I was preaching and demonstrating the miracle power of God while fighting pneumonia in my own body. I had to spend the day in bed in order to preach one time per day. Despite my own condition, God restored many blind, deaf, and lame people to health, even as He brought salvation to many Buddhists.

> ## God hid Himself in His Word
> ## so you can always find Him.

When all sense and knowledge does not bring us comfort, we can still be happy, knowing there is a spoken Word over our life that is greater than our negative feelings. This Word will be a new source of joyful feelings. We decide to become enforcers of that Word and acknowledge through our words its authority in our lives. This Word connection gives our voice an authority that every devil and circumstance must yield to. We are gratified with the results of what we say. The ancient scripture reveals:

> *"A man's belly shall be satisfied with the fruit of his mouth; and with the increase of his lips shall he be filled. Death and life are in the power of the tongue: and they that love it shall eat the fruit thereof."*
> (Proverbs 18:20-21)

Can you use God's Word to deliver yourself?

In a world of many pleasures that lead to vices, it is good to know there is a key to freedom from addictions. A consistent thanks to God acknowledging your freedom, even in the middle of doing your addiction, will bring God onto the scene because He is in His Word. Give constant thanks that His Word declares you free! Jesus is responding to what you say. He said you will know the truth, and the truth will set you free. Did you know that what He says varies according to what you say? Many look for a prophet to speak words of life and blessing over their lives, but you are your own greatest prophet. What you say about yourself IS more important than what anybody else says about you. Even God cannot override what you say about yourself. Jesus reacts in heaven to your words. He takes your words and speaks to the Father based on your words. *"Whosoever therefore shall confess me before men, him will I confess also before my Father which is in heaven. But whosoever shall deny me before men, him will I also deny before my Father which is in heaven."* (Matthew 10:32-33). I know it is amazing, but Jesus is responding to what you say.

What He says about us varies according to what we say. His Words concerning us are affected by our words concerning Him.

Jesus revealed a decision that will occur one day in the future. *"But I say unto you, that every idle word that men shall speak, they shall give account thereof in the day of judgment. For by your words you will be justified and by your words you will be condemned."* (Matthew 12:36)

People who say it does not matter what you say are obviously living on a very short term perspective.

When Jesus shared a story of an unjust man, He revealed that his own words would decide his fate:

> *"And he saith unto him, Out of thine own mouth will I judge thee, thou wicked servant. Thou knewest*

that I was an austere man, taking up that I laid not down, and reaping that I did not sow." (Luke 19:22).

We see in history one of the great Bible stories spoken to children around the world. It is the story of Moses and the deliverance of the children of God from Egypt. It starts off with God hearing the cry of the oppressed that were under the whip of the Egyptians. God responds and sends Moses to deliver them.

They walk out of Egypt after seeing God demonstrate His protection of them over and over from all the plagues on Egypt. They see God deliver them at the Red Sea despite their complaining and their desire to return to bondage for themselves and their children.

Miracle after miracle could not persuade them that God would give them the Promised Land. At the crossing of the river Jordan they sealed their own fate by believing the ten spies who said they could not win and were not able to cross over. The ten spies said the giants looked upon the children of God as grasshoppers. That was far from the truth. Forty years later when the next generation crossed over the river Jordan to Jericho, Rahab the harlot said that all the people of the land were afraid of them because God was with them!

All of God's good plans for them could not work because they said they were not able to cross into the land prepared for them. God told them He will do unto them according to their words, and they all died in the wilderness. Look at what they said that killed the dream of God for their lives.

"And they said unto Moses, because there were no graves in Egypt, hast thou taken us away to die in the wilderness? Wherefore hast thou dealt thus with

203

us, to carry us forth out of Egypt? Is not this the word
that we did tell thee in Egypt, saying, let us alone,
that we may serve the Egyptians? For it had been bet-
ter for us to serve the Egyptians, than that we should
die in the wilderness." (Exodus 14:11-12)

We also get a glimpse of their poor self-image, and their
smallness, from the ten spies who said:

"But the men that went up with him said, we be not
able to go up against the people; for they are stronger
than we." (Exodus 14:31)

What was their problem? They were continually un-
thankful for what was already done for them. They always
assumed the worst and spoke negatively all the time. They
feared that they were not up to the task of conquering the
Promised Land.

Moses had led these people to freedom, but they were
bound inside and could not see what God saw. When the
spies went into the Promised Land a second time 40 years
later, the woman called Rahab said that the people dread-
ed the day when the wandering people would come. Rahab
gave this account:

"And as soon as we heard these things, our hearts
melted; neither did there remain any more courage
in anyone because of you, for the Lord your God,
He is God in heaven above and on earth beneath."
(Joshua 2:11)

The people of Jericho and the Promised Land believed
more about God than the chosen ones! Do we really grasp
the wonderful things that God says about us who are chosen to rule in life?

Faith does the impossible, and the foundation of faith is the known will of God. We still have a choice, even when we know the will of God. Jesus still is working with us confirming His Word and the words we speak in agreement with Him. Paul reminds us to consider the role Jesus is playing right now in our lives as the confirming of what we are saying. He writes:

"Wherefore, holy brethren, partakers of the heavenly calling, consider the Apostle and High Priest of our profession, Christ Jesus." (Heb. 3:1)

Profession means to say the same thing. He agrees with you and works with you when you are in agreement with Him. We are told to keep this in focus during times when nothing seems to be working.

"Seeing then that we have a great high priest, that is passed into the heavens, Jesus the Son of God, let us hold fast our profession (what we say). *For he is faithful that promised."* (Hebrews 4:14)

Our words can be productive or destructive. We have an opportunity to have potent results, but it will take awareness of all that has been done for you, and thankfulness. Paul gives us this insight when he pens that our words work when they reflect the good things that God has done in our lives:

"That the communication of thy faith may become effectual by the acknowledging of every good thing which is in you in Christ Jesus." (Philemon 1:6)

If we choose to complain, curse, or just remain in a negative vocabulary, then the devil will be glad to be in agreement with those words and help bring about destruction.

Christianity concedes to a new reality. We admit that healing in us is real. We admit that abundance exists in us. We
admit that the life we see now is temporary, and then call
those things which be not as though they are. The first step
of a new reality is to acknowledge the kingdom of God in
us, and His desire to see His kingdom established around
us.

> **Can Jesus be the same in your body**
> **as He was in the body of a Jew 2,000 years ago?**
>
> **Yes, if you allow Him!**

As we read God's inspired ideas in His written Word and
act on them, we allow Him to be the same to us as if He
were personally speaking to us. We allow Him to use our
hearts and words to convey His revelation of Jesus' substitution and resurrection to a spiritually empty world — a
world looking for confirmation that God is real and cares
about us!

Why do God's words have life on our lips? Because we have
been resurrected with Christ, and we now sit in the same
place of authority that He sits in.[124] We sit together with
Him.

Jesus does not pace back and forth in front of the throne
wondering if He did enough. He does not worry about
whether we will complete His mission. We read that we are
called to enter into the rest of faith, expecting those things

---

[124] Eph. 1:20, 2:6

which we feel strongly about, think upon, and speak of to come to pass.

What Does God Want From Us?

Jesus believes in us. Why would He sit resting in faith, expecting His enemies to be made His footstool, unless He knew we could do it?[125] We are a new breed of people with His resurrection life in us. That life allows us, like Him, to sit in the rest of faith, expecting answers to our requests.[126]

Since Jesus believes in us, we should believe in ourselves. We should not be nervous, worried, or doubtful of His willingness to give us all He has provided. We should be confident that He will do through us what He began to do when He walked the earth as our model for ministry.

The Apostle Paul wrote the following about our new position in Christ.

> *"But God, who is rich in mercy, for his great love wherewith he loved us, even when we were dead in sins, hath quickened us together with Christ, (by grace ye are saved;) and hath raised us up together, and made us sit together in heavenly places in Christ Jesus."* (Ephesians 2:4-6)

Our being raised up with Christ presupposes that Jesus was quickened in the tomb, and that we were quickened in the grave of our sins.

We can allow God to be the same in us as He was in Jesus, because God has recreated us with a resurrected life force. After we leave this body, it will be obvious to us who we

[125] Heb. 10:12–13
[126] Heb. 4:2–3

really are and what we are capable of accomplishing. It is our privilege, however, to discover these things even now as we live in our perishable bodies.

When we know our exalted position, seated in heavenly places in Christ, we will identify more with the Christ who walked out of the tomb than with the Christ, who died on the Cross.

How Can We Identify With a Resurrected Person?

After His resurrection, Jesus breathed into humanity the same life He has. He stands alone as the only spiritual leader in all of history who energizes His followers with the same life that energizes Him. He alone tells His followers to do the same miraculous signs He did so that people can see that He is alive.

This resurrection life has freed multitudes from a death sentence. In a Russian tent meeting, a man named Anatoly told us of his release from a 12-year drug addiction. This new freedom then ushered in the restoration of his marriage, and a miraculous report from his doctors that he has no evidence of the AIDS virus that he had been afflicted with. This resurrection life, this new reality, goes even to the depths of your DNA if need be, to give you a new start in life!

Remember: When you accept Jesus as your Savior and Lord, you are given a seat with Him in Heaven's chair. And you are empowered by Him to be His representative in the earth. See yourself seated in Christ! When you do, your problems and circumstances will not be towering over you. They will be far beneath you!

CHAPTER 5

THE CHAIR OF FAVOR

The Creator is favoring all in giving all gifts.

What gifts do all believers get?

What is the gift of a new spirit? What are the limits of imagination? Is language the gift that keeps giving?

He Sat Down So We Could Stand Up!

You have not picked up this book by accident. It is designed to release the gift within you. You no longer have to wait for special gifts to serve God. You do not have to wait for the maturing of the nine gifts of the Spirit to operate in your life before you do something for Him.

Be careful about taking the posture of a bystander, hoping that someday Jesus will call you into the arena and anoint you. This posture of sitting, looking, and waiting reminds me again of the first disciples who watched as Jesus ascended into heaven—much like tourists watched as the space shuttle blasted off from Cape Canaveral. The disciples did not know what to do after Jesus disappeared from their sight. Angels had to appear to them to wake them up. They said to Jesus' followers, *"Why do you stand here staring? He is going to return like He left. Get busy about big Kingdom business until that time."*[127]

You see, the dream Jesus completed is our vision to perform. The price He paid is our platform to participate on. His final act is our first step of action.

Now that you have found your rightful seat in The 12th Chair—Heaven's Chair—stand up and proceed boldly to your destiny!

Why did He sit down?

> **His work was finished!**

Why did He sit down?

> **He had passed His work on to His body on the earth!**

Why did He sit down?

> **He believes we can finish what He began!**

Jesus is not wondering if He said enough or did enough to train mankind for victory. No, He sat down at God's right hand knowing He had done all He could do. There was nothing left for Him to do. He had given the example, paid the price of redemption, given His Word, and sent His Spirit so we could not fail.

Now He calls us to stand up from our chair!

This view of Jesus' position was first penned by the great Apostle Paul:

---

[127] Acts 1:10–11 (author's paraphrase)

"But this man, after he had offered one sacrifice for sins forever, sat down on the right hand of God; from henceforth expecting till his enemies be made his footstool."[128]

God has made us able to stand in our righteousness. He has strengthened our backbone to walk uprightly in dignity. He has put power in our words to overcome darkness and have victory over His enemies, thereby uprooting the root of evil in the world. This is the hour to stand in love and let love reign in authority! Love went through death and came out on the other side. Love has a supreme response.

Love is master of all situations, because it goes beyond the normal reaction to a reality of our heavenly position and source. Love is king of the new resurrected life.

People who encounter Jesus have not changed much in 2,000 years. Unless they are trained through books such as the one in your hands, they begin to just stand and wait for a gift from heaven instead of using the gift of righteousness that has already been given to them (see Rom. 5:17).

They stand in churches and wait for a sermon to inspire them. They stand in schools and wait for an education to anoint them. They stand in seminars and wait for the free gift of a prophetic word to call them out. But there is a real danger in waiting. It is the main cause for the failure of the Church structure today. Inactive people find themselves in a very destructive mode.

If you ask a beekeeper when the most dangerous time is to deal with a hive, he will say that it is when the bees have stopped producing honey and the hive is full. Thousands

---

[128] Heb. 10:12–13

211

and thousands of bees swirling around with no work to do causes great agitation. They begin to look at the beekeeper and each other as enemies. And that is when they begin to sting.

Churches that have lost the larger purpose of outreach begin an inward-spiraling cycle of backbiting, scorn, and criticism. This is destructive to the church and the very people they are called to work with.

The angels are still crying out to people, "Why do you stand here waiting? There is no gifting better than the one you have: to be blessed with the indwelling presence of Jesus Himself. There is no training better than what you have: to be led by the Holy Spirit within. There is no prophecy better than what you have: to declare over your life what Jesus has already done for you, and who you are in Him!"

There is no need to wait for what God has already given. However, there is a need to believe in yourself, and that you are gifted by God Himself to carry out His purpose for your life.

Part 1
WHAT ARE THE GIFTS NOBODY TALKS ABOUT?

When Jesus sat down in heaven, He gave gifts to men. These were not just ministry gifts or spiritual gifts. These are the gifts nobody talks about. And they really equip us to go into the world and face every situation.

These are gifts that no one can take away from you!

These are gifts that require no special anointing!

These are gifts that work all the time and in any place!

In the ancient text, God discloses some major transforming truths in the simplest ways that reveal how dynamic the person is who is created in His image. We get a glimpse of this as we read the Word.

> *"Now to Him who is able to do exceedingly abundantly above all that we ask or think, according to the power that works in us."*[129]

God gave you everything,
but it all came as seeds that you have to plant!

That verse from Ephesians—one of the greatest truths ever put into the hands of man—was inspired by God and written by Paul. It illustrates that the three greatest gifts—a

---

[129] Eph. 3:20 NKJV

new spirit, imagination, and language—are the qualities of human potential that make us most like God in action.

The gift of a new spirit: Salvation

The gift of imagination: Vision

The gift of language: Words

In a nutshell, God has given us the ability to think, dream, envision, and imagine what we could be—and then release it by speaking it. The devil has taken advantage of man's ignorance of his own gifts. He uses these gifts against man by perverting their power, which was meant for good, into a destructive force. In the days of Noah, *"God saw that the wickedness of man was great in the earth, and that every imagination of the thoughts of his heart was only evil continually."*[130]

Imagination leads to passion. What you think about is what you become. The image of God in man was so lost among men that they began acting like animals. Unbridled lust and the law of the jungle, where only the strong survive, became the norm for human behavior. Humans had corrupted their powers so much that God saw no redemption for them, except for Noah and his family.

But God continued to work with man, looking ahead to a new time. Speaking through one of His prophets, He said, *"I will give them one heart, and I will put a new spirit within you; and I will take the stony heart out of their flesh, and will give them a heart of flesh."*[131]

God speaks here of a major change that will happen to peo-

---

[130] Gen. 6:5
[131] Ezek. 11:19

ple. He will not use a band aid to solve humanity's problem. He will totally remove the evil heart of man and give him a new one, providing a fresh start. This brings us to the first gift—a recreated spirit. Let us together examine this gift more closely!

PART 2
WHAT IS THE GIFT OF A NEW SPIRIT?

Our nature cannot be fixed, improved, positively motivated, or disciplined. We are in a totally lost, separated, hellbound, sinful condition until God's life comes into us. God did not need to awaken us. He needed to crucify us so a new resurrected being could arise with the same Spirit that raised Jesus. We had to hang on the cross and identify completely with our Savior.

The power of God comes within us at the new birth. It is the defining moment when we receive Jesus as Lord of our life that God indwells us. God did not entrust the task of making mankind a new creation to some institution or individual. Just as God breathed on Adam in the Garden of Eden, now Jesus has breathed on us and given us Himself. God would trust our salvation to no one else.

Humans are not in need of repair.
They are in need of resurrection!

The salvation of a spirit is called a gift.

Paul wrote, *"Dear friends, I've dropped everything to write you about this life of salvation that we have in common. I have to write insisting—begging!—that you fight with everything you have in you for this faith entrusted to us as a gift to guard and cherish.*[132]

---

[132] Jude 1:3 Message

The gift of salvation is what makes us like God. He removes the old, sinful inner man and replaces it with a clean, righteous, holy new person. That is why Jesus told one of the most righteous and good men on the planet in that day, Nicodemus, that he must be born again.[133]

Our best cannot save us. But God will save us and give us His life as a gift, if we believe that Jesus is the Lord and only substitute for man's sinful state!

This is the power that raised a dead man, and it comes into you at your new birth. This is the power that created the universe, and it is now working in your body. This is the power that seats you at God's table as part of His household, and a royal member of His family.

Consider that the potential of a new creation in Christ is as far superior to human potential as human potential is superior to animal potential. Humans have the potential to fly airplanes, play melodious tunes on complex instruments, conduct intricate surgical operations, communicate words that create pictures, and plan for events that will occur 5, 10, and some 20 years in the future. None of this lies within the capacity of animals. But, how many people learn how to fly? How many can play an instrument? How many actually become surgeons? In other words, how many actually discover and utilize the fullness of their amazing capacity?

Nothing is impossible to the new creation. Can that be said of everyone? Can any "new creature in Christ" ever know genuine joy and feel complete without discovering and utilizing his or her uniqueness in applications that are truly helpful to others?

---

[133] John 3:1–3

This is not our idea or the idea of any institution. It was God's idea to save us long before we ever thought about it. He believed in us way before we believed in Him. He loved us long before we loved Him.[134]

The three powerful scriptures that follow tell the story of God's great desire and power to lift us up to His nobility, and dignify us with eternal membership in His family. These scriptures bear out this totally life-changing reality!

"But as many as received him, to them He gave power to become the sons [and daughters] of God, even to them that believe on his name: which were born, not of blood, nor of the will of the flesh, nor of the will of man, but of God."[135]

"Therefore if any man [or person] be in Christ, he is a new creature: old things are passed away; behold, all things are become new."[136]

"Who hath delivered us from the power of darkness, and hath translated us into the kingdom of his dear Son."[137]

Without God's Spirit in us, our conscience would be hardened to sin and blinded to the dangers of the fallen world. We would be trapped by any number of schemes and snares that Satan would use against us at his will.

But we have God's Spirit in us. He bears witness with our spirit that we are God's children.[138] Our spirit is the candle

---

[134] Rom. 5:6–8
[135] John 1:12–13
[136] 2 Cor. 5:17
[137] Col. 1:13
[138] Rom. 8:16

of the Lord.[139] In other words, He enlightens us with wisdom in decisions and sensitivity to hidden dangers.

Years ago when I was in Bible school, I borrowed my roommate's car to go to work. I stopped by the shopping mall and parked. Later on when I began to drive away, I heard an inner voice say, "Hit the brakes!" I obeyed, not knowing why. Suddenly, a car came racing from my blind side at 50 miles per hour right into my path!

Fifteen minutes later I was traveling down a two-lane highway. Once more the voice on the inside said, "Hit the brakes!" I decided to obey again. Two seconds after I hit my brakes a 22-car collision happened in front of me. Because I had slowed down, I spared myself and all the vehicles behind me a major accident. The Lord sees the hidden dangers ahead of us!

The power within us is as creative as the force that created the earth. We can direct it through our imagination and our words.

---

[139] Prov. 20:27

Part 3
WHAT ARE LIMITS OF IMAGINATION?

We see God using the gifts He gave us to create the earth:

"In the beginning God created the heaven and the earth. And the earth was without form, and void; and darkness was upon the face of the deep. And the Spirit of God moved upon the face of the waters."[140]

"And the Spirit of God was hovering over the waters."[141]

Why was God's Spirit hovering over the waters? Have you ever considered what He pondered as He went round and round the earth? He was getting a picture of what it could be like![142]

You build a life by building a dream.

Use your imagination to create it!

He saw red flowers. Then He dreamed of yellow and orange colored flowers. He saw palm trees. Then He thought of tall pine trees, some with brown bark and some with white bark. He saw frogs—green frogs, red frogs, tadpoles, and tree frogs. He looked at rock formations and thought some should be granite, some shale, and some soft clay.

---

[140] Gen. 1:1–2
[141] Gen. 1:2 New International Version
[142] Isa. 40:12

It took much meditation, envisioning, and imagination to conjure up the abundance of beauty and variety we now call earth!

After God the Holy Spirit used imagination to create the world, He gave us the gift of imagination to create our world.

When I graduated from Bible school there were no churches waiting for me to come and preach. There were no countries calling on me for the bits of wisdom I had learned. There were no church boards asking me to be a pastor. So I went out to the small city airport near my house, pulled up a chair with a good view of the airplanes as they came and went, and began to dream of flying on those planes as they headed into the sky.

At that point I was starting to build a vision for world travel. Now, after 30 years of traveling to over 60 nations, I can say that the dream at the beginning has become the reality of today.[143] Let us spend a few moments investigating seven ways to make your dreams come to pass.

I believe all humans have a divine seed of greatness in them. God would not create someone without value or purpose on the inside. He has given us "dream seeds" that we call promises.

Jeremiah wrote, *"Thy words were found, and I did eat them; and thy word was unto me the joy and rejoicing of mine heart: for I am called by thy name, O Lord God of hosts."*[144]

---

[143] Eccl. 7:8

[144] Jer. 15:16

221

Today, we stir up your gift!

Today, we resurrect your dreams!

Today, we discover great ideas!

Many people let their dreams die, or they push them down, or they allow others to talk them out of them. Some people permit bad things such as divorce, bankruptcy, or illness to kill their dreams.

Do you recognize the importance of your dreams? Many dismiss them because they dismiss themselves. Many do not value their dreams because they do not value themselves.

Moses once had a dream of delivering his people, but time and failure ripped it from his heart. God resurrected it, but Moses still had to fight with his own self-image. Some sources say he stammered and his brother Aaron started out being the spokesman.[145] Gideon was called a mighty man of valor by the angel who visited him, but he saw himself as the lowest man of the lowest tribe of Israel.[146] Jeremiah was called to proclaim to the king the destiny of the nation, but he lacked confidence because of his age.[147]

Do not let life, people, failure, or your present condition stop you from keeping the seed of a dream in your heart. The only one who has no dream is the devil. He does not wake up excited. He never wakes up thinking of building something. He never considers improving, loving, or growing anything. Why not? Because he has no future. The devil is a loser. He is limited. He is a liar!

---

[145] Exod. 4:10–16
[146] Judges 6:12, 15
[147] Jer. 1:5–6

You have a great future with unlimited faith, potential, and truth to fall back on in tough times. God has good plans for you! Grab hold of the little thoughts tugging at your heart of what you would like to see or have happen in your life. When you read what the Lord says about you in the Bible, something will ignite inside you![148]

It does not matter how bad your past is. You might say your sins are as dark as mud, but even a glass of mud will become drinkable if you keep pouring clean, fresh water into it. Remember that even a field of weeds will produce corn if you start putting new seeds into the soil!

Here are seven things that will help you make your dreams come to pass:

1. Know you are not alone.

How can you know your dream is in agreement with God? When it produces peace and brings out the best in you. Ask yourself these three questions: Is it good for God? Is it good for people? Is it good for me? If the answers are yes, then go for it!

Ask yourself if you feel good about the thing you are asking of God. Does it stimulate you to imagine? Does it energize you to go after it? If it does, then know that these are qualities of God that are telling you to go after it. Knowing that you have a partner who will help you make your dream happen produces confidence in you. God's will is not a mystery. It is not drudgery or a sacrifice. It is the best thing you could ever do!

---

[148] Jer. 29:11–14

2. Speak your dream to yourself.

You are your best prophet. You know the future because you speak the future. If you don't believe in yourself, then how can you expect others to believe in you?

Use your words to bring up what is in your heart. Your words are signposts pointing to where you are going. They indicate what you are willing to commit to and pay the price to have it in your life.

3. Find out what it will cost for your dream to come to pass.

Jesus told us to consider the cost before we start building.[149] I remember a mistake I made in this area with a yard project. I started digging a 40-foot (12 meters) hole in my front yard for a driveway. After I had made about 50 trips with a wheelbarrow full of dirt, my enthusiasm for building a driveway started to slip away. Enthusiasm can carry you for a while, but accuracy in details is what carries you across the finish line of your dream.

Study, preparation, and continued focus are necessary parts of the picture of your dream. Facts can change, and new ways of doing things may need to be discovered. So you have to keep your focus in the midst of a changing landscape.

4. Find someone to agree with you.

No load is too heavy when you have a friend to help you carry it. You do not need a whole audience to cheer you on. One friend clapping is better than a gallon of water on a walk through the desert!

---

[149] Luke 14:28

Mary had a word from an angel that she would be a virgin mother. She could find no one to really believe that would happen until she went to her cousin Elizabeth, who herself had become pregnant in a miraculous way. The baby in Elizabeth's womb leapt when Mary showed up. Don't hang around people who do not make your unseen baby-vision leap when you talk to them!

5. Don't discuss your dream with those who could kill it.

More dreams have died at the doorstep of a skeptical friend than in front of an army of enemies!

6. Discover the best role models who have succeeded in that field.

Revelation can be caught quickly when the eye is imprinted. It is true that one picture is more valuable than a thousand words. Find someone doing what you want to do and look at them, and you will build your life on the shoulders of success.

Leslie in Sofia, Bulgaria

This truth was confirmed to me during our outdoor miracle events in Eastern Europe. While standing in the rain and mud on a dirt field in Bulgaria, I met one of the most popular motivational speakers of America. I asked him why he would show up at such a humble setting.

Learn from those who have proven to be the best in their respective fields. At that time, this man was considering beginning foreign mass-miracle evangelism. We and Dr. T.L. Osborn were actively involved in doing this very thing. This man said he had a dream of miracle evangelism birthing in his heart, and he wanted to learn. He knew of the ministry Dr. Osborn was doing and wanted to feel it, see it, and absorb it so it could be duplicated in his own future.

This man suffered through ten days of rain with us. Despite the foul weather, the people came out and God confirmed His Word. I admired this man's resolve to imprint his imagination for change. He was marking his thought patterns so he could begin to move in a new direction.

7. Let time be your friend, not your enemy.

Most dreams are not lost to economic circumstances or people's unbelief. Time without evidence of fulfillment can bring confusion into the dream. Confusion steals confidence and brings you into the realm of doubt. Doubt ties the hands of your friend Jesus so He cannot help you in your pursuit.

Deal with time by not considering the past at all, and not thinking about the things you have no control over. Use your time to focus on what you want to have happen and what step you can take today in that direction. God brings about our future and forgets our past!

Two lumberjacks were each given an ax for a day to cut down trees. One was paid twice as much as the other, but he was given one condition: he had to use the flat side of the ax. After a few hours he quit, saying, "I don't care about the money. I have to see the chips fly!"

We all want to see the chips fly. But when they are not flying, we can spend that time sharpening the blade so that when we do have an opportunity, our cut will be deeper! Let time work for you. Develop, train, practice, and pray—knowing that your day will come!

Over the years I have seen other very successful men and women use this same key. An example of this happened to my wife, Leslie, and me in 1998. We raised the first tent in our 100-tent project to reach the millions of people in Eurasia. (Visit www.klmcnulty.net for more information.)

227

Before that tent went up, we did our research. We visited several tent factories and walked through many tents of others to understand and envision what we would need. Now, we are well on the way to completion of these 100 tents. With teams going strong, we continue to move closer to our goal of having an evangelist, team, and tent in every newly opened country, republic, and oblast of Eurasia.

It took a lot of dreaming, contemplating, and study to build a successful program for a traveling tent ministry—especially after two attempts by other ministries had failed!

It also took a lot of determination. The first tent was bought out from under us before we could put our hands on it. The first offering was taken back. The first fundraiser lost money. The first pastors' gathering was a flop. But then the breakthrough happened when favor shined out of the dark onto our project.

The gift of imagination is given to you to cause the dream of your heart to come to pass. It is easy to squander this gift through thoughts that are distracting, anxious, or foolish. These will try to fill your mind.

It takes a real decision to guard your mind so that it is not overwhelmed by the abundance of voices and pictures that are constantly at our fingertips in our modern society. Let us fill our minds with the visions of where we really want to go, and what we really want to be five and ten years from now. If you do not plan what port your ship will go to, then it does not matter if you have a rudder to steer. Do not just let the winds of circumstance and chance drive you. Set sail with a destination in mind.

> **Solomon said it simply: "Forsake the foolish, and live; and go in the way of understanding."[150]**

Don't just exist on this planet and mark time, **LIVE!** If you can control your thoughts, you can overcome in life. No person, spirit, or circumstance has the right or ability to control your thoughts. You are the master of your inner man! You are the captain of your soul. If all else is stripped from you, nothing can strip the most important thing—your soul. Jesus said your soul is worth more than the whole world. So learn to nurture and protect it by deciding what thoughts you will think.

"What good is it for someone to gain the whole world, yet forfeit their soul?"[151]

The spirit of a prophet is subject to the prophet. You are your own prophet. Therefore your voice is the primary one you should listen to. You prophesy your own future every day by the words you speak in faith. The more your thoughts, dreams, and imagination take you in a certain direction, the more you will talk about it and build faith for it to happen. Given enough time, that thing which you have imagined (whether good or bad) will come to pass.

A glimpse of our gifts at work!

Think about the ancient people mentioned in the Book of Genesis who wanted to build a tower to Heaven in a place

---

[150] Prov. 9:6
[151] Mark 8:36 NIV 2011

eventually called Babel. God said that nothing they imagined would be impossible for them.[152]

This is a very clear picture of man's gifts at work, even if in a wrong way. It is interesting that Jesus used the same language, saying nothing shall be impossible to us who believe. I believe it is worth looking at these ancient people of Babel who did the impossible, even though:

• **They did not have** a covenant with God, but YOU DO!

• **They did not have** the written Word of God, but YOU DO!

• **They did not have** the Holy Spirit, but YOU DO!

• **They did not have** a sacrifice permanently removing their sins, but YOU DO!

• **They did not have** access to a church, pastor, books, websites, DVDs, and CDs, but YOU DO!

Their story is important because it shows that God put gifts within all men, and they could use them to their benefit or to their destruction. It shows that dreams do not come to pass because a person is special or has a special anointing, but because of a gift that God put in all people.

This is their story . . .

"And the whole earth was of one language, and of one speech. And it came to pass, as they journeyed from the east, that they found a plain in the land of Shinar; and they dwelt there. And they said one to another, Go to, let us make brick, and burn them

---

[152] Gen. 11:6

thoroughly. And they had brick for stone, and slime had they for mortar. And they said, Go to, let us build us a city and a tower, whose top may reach unto heaven; and let us make us a name, lest we be scattered abroad upon the face of the whole earth. And the Lord came down to see the city and the tower, which the children of men builded. And the Lord said, Behold, the people is one, and they have all one language; and this they begin to do: and now nothing will be restrained from them, which they have imagined to do."[153]

God was angry at them, not for building a tower, but for something more serious. They had chosen to walk away from His calling to be fruitful, multiply, and fill the earth.[154] Even at the beginning God had the whole earth on His mind. However, these people would not go. They wanted to stay and build something that everybody could live within eyesight of.

I like what Scripture has to say about these totally disadvantaged people. They were one, so they had the power of similar vision. This means they were all going in the same direction. Now that was real agreement operating in their midst!

Jesus gives us a glimpse of our rights under the new covenant by saying that if two of us will agree on anything on earth, it shall be done.[155]

God says they were speaking the same thing. There were no tongues of criticism, defeatism, or worry among them.

---

[153] Gen. 11:1–6
[154] Gen. 1:28
[155] Matt. 18:19–20

Everybody was waking up ready to work toward a great goal.

So they began to work. Wow! Nobody waited for blue skies, better tools, or a boss to tell them to work. Here is an of-ten-overlooked secret to success:

God gets involved when we get involved!

Why can Christians sometimes appear to be limited? Is it because we do not act like one people? Or speak the same thing? Or have the same vision?

It is exciting to know that, according to Jesus, when these simple forces are at work in our lives, nothing shall be impossible for us!

The same principles that worked for a group in the Old Testament will work for an individual believer in the New Testament. According to your faith-filled imagination, language, and action, it will be done for you!

Part 4
IS LANGUAGE THE GIFT THAT KEEPS GIVING?

We all love to talk, but talking is more than just making noise. Animals make noise. They grunt, screech, howl, and make unique sounds for mating, danger, or hunting—all based on the instincts they have been given by God.

Do not confuse these instinctive sounds with the ability God has given humans. He has honored us with the power to create our own world by drawing portraits with our words. The pictures we paint with our words draw favor, blessings, goodwill, love, healing, finances, and trust to us. We also can draw anger, hate, fear, anxiety, and death into our lives by what we continually say about ourselves.

> **As coins are the currency of earth, words spoken in faith are the currency of Heaven!**

Words are so important in the economy of the kingdom of God that our life for eternity is based on what we say! Salvation is based on what we believe in our hearts and say with our mouths concerning Jesus Christ.[156] We are speaking spirits in earth bodies. The body gives the spirit man a right to speak the things of the unseen spirit realm into the seen realm. The Scriptures say, *"Death and life are in the power of the tongue: and they that love it shall eat the fruit thereof."*[157]

---

[156] Rom. 10:10
[157] Prov. 18:21

Jesus said that when we stand before Him someday, we will have to explain why we said certain words:

"O generation of vipers, how can ye, being evil, speak good things? For out of the abundance of the heart the mouth speaketh. A good man out of the good treasure of the heart bringeth forth good things: and an evil man out of the evil treasure bringeth forth evil things. But I say unto you, that every idle word that men shall speak, they shall give account thereof in the day of judgment. For by thy words thou shalt be justified, and by thy words thou shalt be condemned."[158]

Our own words will either justify or condemn us—so it really does matter what we say! An old friend of my family's—who was a hard-drinking, cursing man almost all his life—experienced Christ gloriously in a church service and had a spiritual new birth. He was so sensitive to the presence of Jesus within him that when he tried to speak, all he could do was nod his head, because his whole vocabulary consisted of curse words. It took him six months before he could say a sentence without cursing! Jesus said we bring up blessings or curses from our heart and release them with our words.

We must be sensitive to what we are saying. People want to speak their minds. That is a good thing unless what is in their minds does not match up with their place in God's Kingdom, their rights as God's children, their privileges as members of God's family, or their love dominion based on their legal standing with God. They talk as if they are not redeemed. They talk as if they are not free from the curse of death and the fear of injury, sickness, accidents, plagues, and evil men that bring death.

---

[158] Matt. 12:34–37

234

Do not waste your precious gift

Do not waste your precious gift of speech by declaring that you are in agreement with evil, failure, depression, sickness, or fear. Even if it looks as if the economy is going into depression, you do not have to go into depression with it, because you know and believe that you have a source that cannot be touched by man. You may see the evil work of killers, thieves, and corrupt men in the streets or at the highest levels of government, but you do not have to participate in their destruction.

In the back of their minds, those people might be thinking they are getting away with it. Cheaters, liars, manipulators, and evil men might appear to be living a better life by the shortcuts they take. The reality is that without peace, there is no better life. Humans have been designed to live in peace only when they have peace with God.

Scripture says that for the wicked there is no rest. Of course, if they can no longer think and they lie down in a stupor, they will sleep. But when they put their heads on their pillows at night and consider the results of their actions, there is no sleep. There is fear of the destruction that is coming because they know they have sown a life of evil words. They are simply time bombs waiting to explode.

We speak a new language of hope with the expectation of good things happening, because we are connected to a new source of life. Our peace is not tied to the stock market or our investments, employers, or politicians. Rather, it is linked to our Savior, who is the Peacemaker of the world!

When God created man, He gave him a job. Adam was told to name all the animals. He also was given authority over the earth and everything on it. So, when Adam gave some-

235

thing a name, it had to respond to him because he was the one in authority. When he called for it, it had to come because he was the one who named it.

Because of Jesus, all people can now understand their honored, royal place of authority on earth. The Bible says that at the name of Jesus, everything on earth, under the earth, and in heaven will bow its knee, and every tongue will confess that He is Lord.[159] That name is the authorized authority recognized in all realms. Scripture tells us to use that name in prayer and use that name to defeat our enemies.

When Jesus burst through the gates of hell and paraded Satan around the earth as a defeated foe, He took the keys of hell and death. Jesus put mankind on notice that authority in the earth had been given back to them. He told Peter that whatever he bound on earth would be bound in heaven, and whatever he loosed on earth would be loosed in heaven.[160] Believers were given back the keys of authority on the earth, and those keys are words. Jesus said, *"The words I have spoken to you are spirit and they are life."*[161]

When you are speaking, if you are not connecting with your spirit and your soul, your words can be empty and nonproductive. If you are acting in some repetitious, religious manner and not engaging your thoughts and your feelings with your words, you cannot expect the seed of your words to bear fruit. This could be why some people have faith failures. If you are speaking God's words with faith, there is no reason to feel shameful or fearful.

---

[159] Phil. 2:10–11
[160] Matt. 16:19
[161] John 6:63 NIV 1984

Some old institutions challenge me over why we put up the big tents in the former Soviet Union. Some old institutions rose up and called us a cult, or worse. We are not afraid of the open arena where thoughts can be spoken and debated. I will gladly put up a tent for my opposition as well as myself, and let the people decide whom they want to listen to. People are smart. They know when someone is speaking from the heart. They know in their own hearts who to listen to!

People are intelligent. They would rather follow a living prophet than a dead one. We have the words of life that God confirms, and He manifests the same results in our lives that He manifested in the life of Jesus. When these words are spoken, heard, and received with faith, then the people will see transformations in spirit, soul, and body!

Faith is to humans in the spiritual environment what oxygen is to humans in the ocean environment.

CHAPTER 6

THE CHAIR OF FAITH

- **What is faith?**
- **How does faith work?**
- **What brings out our best results?**
- **What are the three supernatural seeds of faith?**

What is Jesus looking for? When He returns will He find faith? (Luke 8:18)

Faith is what Jesus is looking for!

If we take scripture at face value, it is clear that **Faith is** God's expectation of humanity. An active trust in God's Word is based on the finished work that Jesus Himself accomplished. When a man with an epileptic son came to Jesus for a miracle, the man asked if Jesus could do anything. Jesus immediately responded, *"Everything is possible for one who believes."*(Mark 9:23)

The problem is not with Jesus! He is able. He is willing, and He is ready, but He wants to know if you believe He will do it.

> *"For in Christ, neither our most conscientious religion nor disregard of religion amounts to anything.*

239

What matters is something far more interior: faith expressed in love." (Galatians 5:6, Message)

This faith works within the framework of love. Love is the foundation. GOD'S LOVE provides the motive for our confident belief.

We trust God because we know He is a loving God. Love was here long before contracts and covenants. Love is a selfless willingness to do good and right for all. The impossible can spring from this foundation.

PART 1
DEFINING FAITH

FAITH IS how we CONDUCT OUR LIFE.

FAITH IS a lifestyle we are all called to live. Three times in the New Testament it says, *"The just shall live by faith."* (Rom. 1:17; Gal. 3:11; Heb. 10:38). What does that mean? It signifies that our decisions are not just based on our senses. It will require steps to be made without having all the facts, resources, or people in place, but God will make the difference. We rest in that.

FAITH IS a LOOK.

FAITH IS the window by which we see all that God has done for us.

We cannot go further than we can see. **Faith is** a way of looking at life with a long perspective. It is also a way of looking at the present, knowing it will change. The Apostle Paul wrote, *"We look not at the things which are seen, but at the things which are not seen: for the things which are seen are temporal; but the things which are not seen are eternal"* (2 Cor. 4:18). And the writer of Hebrews said, *"Now faith is the substance of things hoped for, the evidence of things not seen"* (Heb. 11:1). We have an inner eye that can see things as God sees them if we allow ourselves to view our world this way. Faith gives us a picture of the future.

FAITH IS a RESPONSE.

241

All that our Creator gave is now ours. We are responders to His undeserved, unearned favor on our lives. We do not put off to a future date receiving what He has already provided by His redemptive work. His finished work is enough. Our work is to respond by receiving His work. And His work paid for our desires. Paul put it this way: *"By grace are ye saved through faith; and that not of yourselves: it is the gift of God: not of works, lest any man should boast"* (Eph. 2:8–9).

FAITH IS an unconscious KNOWING.

Some work hard at talking about faith, yet never see the fruit of it. We start life out with a clean slate, then we begin to learn. We start our Christian lives knowing we are saved and going to heaven. We know our sins are forgiven and expunged from our being. We know that Christ is living in us. Our knowing keeps growing as the written Word is revealed to us. That Word says, *"Faith comes by hearing, and hearing by the word of God"* (Rom. 10:17 NKJV). What do we hear? The things that are written. The Apostle John wrote, *"These things have I written unto you that believe on the name of the Son of God; that ye may know that ye have eternal life, and that ye may believe on the name of the Son of God"* (1 John 5:13).

Faith paints a picture of a better, more complete, fulfilling life. It gives us a model to follow and a standard to reach for, despite the difficulties, culture, color, or education of the present moment. To see results or great change in life, we must make a decision, and then we must practice the life that our new view says is ours. Musicians must practice to harmonize. Sportsmen must practice to win competitions. Christians practice their faith in God by holding to the biblically-based attitude that He has already made them victorious in Christ and that He will answer their prayers.

Unfortunately, rather than having a light, joyful, expressive life, many Christians are burdened by their faith. Most songs they sing are about the weights, persecutions, and troubles they have on earth. They are not about the wonderful, redeemed, victorious life of righteousness God has given them. The songs tell us to hang on because it will be better on the other side. Is a life of faith a hard, troubling walk of sorrows? Are we to just hold on and wait for it to be better on the other side? Is that God's plan? Is that the life Jesus paid for with His life? Is that the victory over the devil, the world, and the flesh that Jesus won? No! John wrote, *"This is the victory that has overcome the world — our faith"* (1 John 5:4 NKJV).

When you are seated in the Chair of Faith, you sit in a confident rest of faith, even as Jesus has completed His work and now sits at the right hand of God. We are to be diligent in our work to enter into the rest of faith. This is God's directive to us. The writer of Hebrews said, *"To whom was God speaking when he vowed that they would never enter his place of rest? He was speaking to those who disobeyed him. So we see that they were not allowed to enter his rest because of their unbelief. . . . So there is a special rest still waiting for the people of God. For all who enter into God's rest will find rest from their labors, just as God rested after creating the world. Let us do our best to enter that place of rest. For anyone who disobeys God, as the people of Israel did, will fall"* (Heb. 3:18–19, 4:9–11 NLT 1996).

Many read this as a difficult New Testament task. Our work, or fight, is not to obey the laws, but to foster an awareness of Christ's finished work in having given us His best. His work is now exalted, magnified, and focused upon us; so joy, laughter, and inspiration flow out of our inner man. We are not pacing back and forth in front of the throne of God in prayer worrying if we have done enough. Jesus is not pacing back and forth in the court of heaven wondering if He needs to do more sacrifice. Sin and its children of guilt and shame have been removed from mankind. With this new life source we are able to resist the plague of doubt in society and to foster a rest of faith.

The devil is an enemy, but a defeated one. He has no power to reign unless that power was given by a human. He is not our battlefield. We do not war with the devil just like we do not war with Jamaica or the Bahamas. They are not in a position to be an opponent. They do not carry a position that would ever warrant America going to war with them. There is no possibility of defeat and no real threat they could have on us. We need not raise the devil's position to a combatant. He is a loser, a liar, and limited. He only needs to be cast out.

God is not responding to our nervous anxiety. When we examine the heroes of faith, we conclude that they were confident in the realm in which they needed faith to work. Faith is the realm in which unseen things are more real than visible things. Faith is the substance of things hoped for, and the evidence of things unseen. (See Heb. 11:1.)

Jesus sat down because His work was finished. Our work is not finished yet, but we rest in His work as we go into our world to establish the kingdom of God.

FAITH IS to humans on earth what oxygen is to scuba divers. Only fish call the ocean their environment. If you do not have oxygen, you cannot function in the water. How long can a diver without oxygen tanks survive under water? Only a matter of minutes.

In the same way, this earth is not our natural environment. We try to put all sorts of laws, contracts, medicines, and insurances in place to protect us, but it still is a hostile world. As long as we are here, we must strap on our faith tanks to enjoy the world we are living in. God provides tanks filled with grace, salvation, redemption, new resurrection life, and ability to live like Christ our model, so we can breathe in the fresh air of His life. Let's take all we know about Jesus and understand about God and apply it to our daily lives. As we do, we will build a solid future in this earthly realm. And we will prepare ourselves to move to our natural realm in heaven.

PART 2

HOW FAITH WORKS

Let us now look at the operation of this dynamic called faith. We see many Biblical examples of ordinary people living in the free, open air of God's powerful redemptive truth. Peter the Apostle told the beggar by the gate of the temple, *"Look at us."*

> *"When he saw Peter and John about to enter, he asked them for some money. Peter and John looked at him intently, and Peter said, 'Look at us!' The lame man looked at them eagerly, expecting some money. But Peter said, 'I don't have any silver or gold for you. But I'll give you what I have. In the name of Jesus Christ the Nazarene, get up and walk!' "*[162]

Focus more on what you have than on what you do not have! Peter and John knew they were the ones with answers for hurting humanity. *Look on us! Look on us!* Wow, this is not religion talking, this is creative Christianity in action! It is not a common thought anymore, but as a Christian you can tell needy, hurting people to look at you. You have the answer to their problem. It may not appear that you have it, and it may not come in the form they were wanting or expecting, but you have the answer.

When the Church stopped taking responsibility for producing answers, then governments and other institutions started saying, "Look at us." This relinquishing of responsibility for receiving miracle supply has caused the Body of Christ to slip into a corner of the world's influence when

---

[162] Acts 3:3–6 NLT

the Creator has said that we are to be center stage. *"The church, you see, is not peripheral to the world; the world is peripheral to the church. The church is Christ's body, in which he speaks and acts, by which he fills everything with his presence"* (Eph. 1:23 Message).

What is our challenge? Time.

God has given us all that pertains to life, and we have the answers. We have a source that cannot be controlled by other humans, economics, armies, or any powers. People are excited when they hear the voice of God's Scripture declare that all things are theirs to enjoy. It is God telling them to enter the supermarket and fill up their basket as often as they like. They go into the store with joy, but they are dismayed when everything they want is packaged as bags of seed. It's not in the form they were looking for. God promises us apples, but He rarely, if ever, gives us orchards or even a single apple tree. He gives us apple seeds.

People want instant gratification. The seeds God gives will produce everything they want in life, but they must plant them. The seeds will produce the image they project. They will grow. They will multiply just like any other seeds. God's words are self-fulfilling. Jesus' words are pre-programmed to produce the images of you and your life that He bought and paid for. His words are self-fulfilling in your life. A tomato seed is pre-programmed to produce tomatoes. It does not matter how much the tomato seed would like to produce potatoes or how long it tries to grow them. It can only produce what it was programmed for.

Whatever seeds from God's storehouse we plant, we will have the same harvest as God Himself would receive if He planted them. Humans are unique in God's creation in their ability to speak words. Seed promises are words.

247

Words are energy. Spoken words are directed energy. No animal can change another animal. They can grunt and chirp and roar, but they have no creative language to transform another. Monkeys are doing the same thing today they were doing 2,000 years ago. We are not of the animal species but of the God species. The status of our new life in Christ is as superior to our old life as human life is superior to animal life. God has given us who are created in His image the ability to transform others. How? By the creative power of the words we speak. We have seen multitudes of people change from sad to glad, from depressed to joyful, from sick to healthy, from lost to saved, from fearful to faithful, from worried to peaceful, and from every other negative state to a positive one. These changes occurred after they heard and believed the words and thoughts of God.

On the border of Romania in the Carpathian Mountains, we were holding tent meetings that were transforming every strata of society. The associate mayor was so touched he gave the unused sports center to the church for their new building so youth could find Christ. A gang of boys came in one day to break up our benches and disrupt the meetings. The leader was going to give the signal when to start the disruption, so they all sat, waiting in anticipation. Sitting there in the presence of the Word, they felt a strong pull to give their lives to Jesus. When the gang leader stood up to give the signal to start trouble, he instead came forward to be born again. The gang all came forward and three weeks later at the baptism service on the river they all jumped into the river together to be baptized, then began sharing amazing stories of transformation with us!

YOUR WHISPER WILL CREATE a WONDER

It is not the loudness or length of speaking that produces change; it is the words that are spoken. For example, we were in the capital of Costa Rica with a marvelous group of leaders and believers, as well as thousands of other people.

Kevin preaching in San Jose, Costa Rica

We conducted over 21 meetings. We met with the president of the country. The national Christian television station broadcast all the meetings across Latin America. Our time there was building to a climax, when our interpreter decided he was tired and wasn't coming to my final meeting.

Tired?? One doesn't get tired in the middle of a campaign! I found myself at the meeting with the music playing, 40,000 people waiting to hear the Word of God and be healed, and no interpreter.

What would you do? What you believe really comes out in moments like this. I told the choir to keep singing and I walked among the people looking for someone who could speak English. I found an old schoolteacher. He had a whisper of a voice, but he could speak accurately. I told him not to worry. "I will preach with heart," I said. "Just say the words, and Jesus will back us up. Only be accurate with the words."

249

My faith was in Jesus alone, and it was very lonely up there with the multitude waiting to see Jesus. My dear new friend whispered the message, and I prayed with great vigor for the manifestation of the healing power of God to make the people whole. My friend whispered the prayer, but it brought a great thunder of faith from their hearts and miracles began to flow. Many canes and wheelchairs were thrust into the air. Arms were lifted, and a parade of hurting humanity gave witness to the living God.

The next day in the town where I was staying, I was negotiating with an art store owner for a particular painting. He greeted me with a big smile and called me Pastor. I had never mentioned that I was a preacher, how did he know?

He said his wife had insisted that he go to the mass miracle meeting the previous night, and so he had stood way in the back. When I invited people to lay hands on themselves where they would like Jesus to lay His hand, he could not think of anything wrong except the golf-ball-size bone deformity he was born with on his lower spine. As he touched it, he felt it dissolve under his hand. He was so happy that Jesus revealed Himself, and he found Christ on that field. I have the picture that we haggled over hanging in our home today.

The Dynamic Seed

Do you know the parts of a seed? There are three. First is an outer husk--a hard, permanent shell. Second is the inner meat. And third is the germ or life spark. Science has been able to duplicate the outer shell and the inner meat but not the germ.

It's important to comprehend how the seed works in order to comprehend how faith works. The outer shell is for protection and permanence. In the realm of faith, it represents the permanent parameter of truth. It is the known will of God. Apart from the known will of God there is no Bible faith. This is like the boundary on a basketball court. The game will continue until the ball goes out of bounds and the referee blows the whistle. When the whistle is blown, all play stops. Like the game on the court, Biblical faith cannot operate outside the bounds or the known will of God. And His will is revealed in the words, example, and finished redemptive work of Jesus Christ.

> ## "Faith can only begin where the will of God is known."
> ## – F. F. Bosworth

The inner matter or meat of the seed is what the germ feeds on. You could say that your spiritual life is feeding on the ideas, inspirations, concepts, and wisdom of Scripture that daily nurtures you or builds you up.

The third part of the seed, the germ, has the life force that is the creative power making it all happen. In science we would call this a dynamo, or self-starting and self-sustaining energy. In the spiritual realm, this is the same life that resurrected Jesus in the tomb. It is the new source of life not limited to the earthly realm. When we say yes to God's plan, our "yes" acts as a catalyst that sets in motion all the unmerited favor of the Creator for His creation. Our positive expectation mixes with truth and creates the desired result.

POSTURE YOURSELF for YOUR PURPOSE

Jesus was completely God. He was as much God at the age of one as He was at the age of thirty-three. No one recognized who He was when He was very young, but all saw the signs of God when He was mature. Like Jesus, we also are made in God's image, but we need to grow in order to mature into the likeness of Christ so the world can see Him operate on the earth. God is Spirit, but now people are His flesh. How does that growth happen? Is it by luck, gifting, or special selection? No, it comes by understanding who Jesus is, who we are, and what our purpose is in life. We take this knowledge to the marketplace of life and see it work.

> *"If ye be Christ's, then are ye Abraham's seed, and heirs according to the promise. Now I say, That the heir, as long as he is a child, differeth nothing from a servant, though he be lord of all; But is under tutors and governors until the time appointed of the father"* *(Gal. 3: 29–4:2).*

As long as we are "immature," the *fact* of *who* we really are and the *reality* of the *power* that resides within us remains concealed from the world, and even from ourselves. Our ignorance *restrains* us—it acts as a governor and keeps us from operating in the realm God intends for us to master. Once we learn, or are tutored in, who and what we are in Christ, the "governor" is no longer necessary.

You don't give your ten-year-old son access to the 12-gauge shotgun you purchased for him until you are confident that he *understands* what he needs to know, and will show the proper *restraint*. That point of understanding is *"the time appointed of the Father."*

When I first seriously committed my life to Christ, I wanted to race to every person I could with the little bit of information I had. It was wonderful! Zeal should not be muzzled, but it does need direction. I was making plans to quit my job when the Lord spoke to me through the prophet Jeremiah. This verse jumped from the page: *"If you have run with the footmen, and they have wearied you, then how can you contend with horses?"* (Jer. 12:5). Jesus needed some time to season me for the work ahead. I needed to grow inwardly as well as communicate outwardly.

Faith is an unconscious result of our determined discovery of Christ in us. Faith is the result of knowing who Jesus is. Once you know who He is, you know who you are. And once you know who you are, you know what you can do.

Grace is the house in which all blessings are paid for and your name is placed on them. Faith is the door to that house. It opens to make available all the life, value, health, dreams, and provision of heaven. A lack of understanding of active believing can keep us from living a full and complete life. Scripture tells us it is impossible to please God without faith.[163] God gives provision, but it must be received. The ancient text says that the just shall live by faith.[164] We are to be thankful responders in life.

When Jesus visited Nazareth, His hometown where He had friends and loved ones, He could do no mighty work there even though He was doing miracles everywhere else. He was among people He especially loved because He grew up with them, but despite Jesus' desire to help them something hindered Him. Something in Nazareth was stronger than God

[163] Heb. 11:6
[164] Hab. 2:4

on the earth. What was it? A secret devil cult? A powerful, evil king or leader? No! The Bible tells us that it was unbelief. It was simply what they thought about Jesus.

Because of the people's unbelief, Jesus could not do any mighty works in His hometown (Mark 6:5). Wow! Does that mean that our unbelief can kill the great potential God has put in our lives? Yes, it does. We are called to live by faith (Rom. 1:17), so we had better understand how faith works! Faith is the master key to a realm where nothing is impossible. It is the key to moving mountains of adversity away from you and bringing mountains of desired blessing toward you.

Nothing really changes in our lives until our beliefs change. Our beliefs can be deep-seated and difficult to change because of our past experiences, feelings, and knowledge. The two ways most people change beliefs are through crisis and through revelation.

It is better to allow new insight, or revelation, to mold and change us than to allow crisis to create negative memories and a distorted self-image. For example, there are so many people sick in modern society that the medical field is consistently one of the top growth industries. Physical crisis can be overcome through faith in the finished work of Christ, but people can close their ears and eyes to this avenue of physical healing. Refusal to hear the living Word and see the life of freedom that Jesus has created is a reason for sickness. We see this warning from Jesus: *"For the hearts of these people are hardened, and their ears cannot hear, and they have closed their eyes—so their eyes cannot see, and their ears cannot hear, and their hearts cannot understand, and they cannot turn to me and let me heal them."* (Matt. 13:15NLV).

Crisis can lift you, or it can create negative experiences, thoughts, and feelings that bring on more crises. In the drama of life you might sometimes find it hard to identify the hand of God. Time will reveal to you a pattern of accidents or accuracy. Many have a life pattern of living from crisis to crisis. That is not God's best. Jesus did say, *"In the world you will have tribulation; but be of good cheer, I have overcome the world."* (John 16:33 NKJV). He is not bringing the tribulation—He is overcoming it with His finished work and He wants you to be happy about it. We are not designed to continually handle hard struggles, difficulty, shame, lack, stress, and failures. Jesus said, *"Come unto me and I will give you rest for your souls."* Jesus said His yoke was easy and His burden light (Matt. 11:28–30). We can take on great conflict and deal with great crisis, but on the inside it must be light and easy or these things will destroy us.

We can help millions understand how to handle crisis by overcoming with joy the crises in our own life. Our victories can be duplicated by others, and therefore, the Kingdom of God will be established.

The Power Of a New Idea

How do we begin to live a life of consistent results? We start with just one new idea. One new thought can change our future. One new idea or word can lift us to a new view. We see a clear example of this in the Biblical story of the rich father's son who took all his inheritance and spent it on wild living.[165] He ended up in a hog pen eating with the pigs. Even at such a low point in life—with feelings of shame, disgust, and self-hatred—this son had one new thought: to go back to his father as a servant.

---

[165] Luke 15:11–24

255

That one new thought brought him into a new life, with his father putting the royal robe on him and giving him a position once again as a son at his table. You're only one thought away from sitting at God's table! Change comes first in your thought life. Begin your tomorrow with a new thought.

New ideas have personally changed my destiny. I have seen it work a number of times in my life, but my beliefs always changed before I changed. The new idea, relationship, or opportunity changed how I thought about myself and my future. My inside changed before my outside did. My desires, focus, and words were all transformed by the new thought. Beliefs must change before results come.

In Scripture we see that a sick woman with a blood disease only got worse for 12 years until she heard of Jesus. She heard something about Jesus that stimulated her to act and reach out to Him. In all those years of illness she never found something to change herself. Then she changed her belief and touched Him, and Jesus said it was her faith that healed her.

Another story is of a Roman centurion who recognized that Jesus had authority in the spirit realm. This military man needed a miracle for another person. When he changed his view of this Jew from Nazareth and acknowledged His power, Jesus said to him, *"As you have believed, so let it be done for you"* (Matt. 8:13 NKJV).

At the age of eleven, **I changed** from a boy without focus to one with drive when a man put a tennis racket in my hand. A desire was birthed in me to be a tennis champion. That desire brought me in my youth to a ranking of 40th in the United States.

I changed again when a Bible was put in my hand and Jesus came into my life. A whole new zeal, focus, and desire to go around the world with a message to help people began. That change of desire brought me to more than 60 nations.

I changed again when I got married at the age of 32 and took on the responsibility and joy of a life shared with another. That change enlarged my life with new dimension.

I changed again when I started to preach and work with Dr. T.L. Osborn on a global scale. I was learning from a master the motivations, philosophy, and power of the Gospel that would move masses of hurting humanity to their answer in Christ.

You do not have to know everything about life to make the most of your time on earth, but there are two things you must know. There are two laws that govern humanity just as much as gravity and other natural laws govern the planet.

PART 3

The Laws that Govern

There are laws that govern God's "moral universe" just as we recognize the laws that govern the physical universe. Cause and effect is used to defend the creation of earth by God. Is there a cause and effect in the realm of faith where actions can predict results? If we have an unchangeable Christ, can we discover principles of His Kingdom that are unchangeable?

The Law of Sowing and Reaping

Paul made this first law clear when he said, *"Do not be deceived, God is not mocked; for whatever a man sows, that he will also reap."*[166] God declared that seedtime and harvest would continue as long as the earth remained (Gen. 8:22). He sowed the seed of His Son to reap the harvest of billions of sons and daughters. **There are two overriding truths here: Seed produces after its own kind. And seed always produces more than the amount of seed sown.**

These truths will work in every area of life. At my home I have terrible bushes that try to overpower my property, and they flourish. If these principles work for bad, corruptible seed like those undesirable bushes, just think how well they will work for an incorruptible seed like the words, thoughts, and actions motivated by your relationship with your Lord!

We are seed planters. Everything in my life; my world, my body, my ministry, my job, and my family begins with a seed.

---

[166] Gal. 6:7 NKJV

258

How much do you want out of life?

How high do you want to climb?

How long do you want to live?

How much power will you exercise?

What goals do you want to reach?

You could say this: whatever you give yourself to will increase. Whatever you put your focus on will multiply. In your life, whatever you pay attention to will grow, and whatever you ignore will diminish. Seeds give back what you plant, and more.

The world's version of this law is, "What goes around, comes around." Jesus told His disciples, *"It has been given to you to know the mysteries of the Kingdom of Heaven."*[167] He then talked for a long time about the life of a farmer. Jesus used the farmer and seed to explain how the Kingdom of God works. The farmer is the example that Jesus used to explain the basic principle that governs life.

The parable of the sower is the foundational truth that Jesus taught. In the book of Matthew you can read it in the 13th chapter, verses 3 through 9. It begins, *"Behold, a sower went out to sow."*[168]

Jesus explained that parable to His disciples in verses 18 through 23. Then He continued teaching about the Kingdom of Heaven, still using a farmer, seed, and sowing to explain His points.

---

[167] Matt. 13:11 NKJV
[168] Matt. 13:3 NKJV

"The Kingdom of Heaven is like a man who sowed good seed in his field."[169]

"The Kingdom of Heaven is like a mustard seed, which a man took and sowed in his field."[170]

Many people, including many preachers, say that God is in control and whatever happens is His will. But does a farmer reap what God sows? What kind of crop will the farmer get if he takes the year off and just tells God he will take whatever crop God produces? How will that work out?

Does the farmer reap what life sows? Is his crop dependent on chance, luck, or destiny? No, the farmer reaps what *he himself* sows. The field will not produce based on the farmer's prayers, or his goodness, or his giving, or anything else. The field will only produce the fruit of the seed that the farmer plants.

What if a farmer had a field, and he kept planting seed for a crop he did not want? Can you picture him going out every day to pull up all the growth he did not want? He would spend days working his vast field, just pulling up plants he did not want. When the field was completely clean, he then would go out and plant more seeds for a crop he did not want. What would you tell this hard working farmer to do? What advice would you give him? We would all agree that we would tell him, "Plant seeds for what you want!"

Isn't it true that everybody everywhere would give this same advice? Why? Because we all know that the field only responds to the seed sown. It does not matter whether the farmer is a good man, a holy man, or a deserving man. It

---

[169] Matt. 13:24 NKJV
[170] Matt. 13:31 NKJV

does not matter whether the farmer promises to feed the poor with the harvest or whether he goes out every day and prays on his knees over the seed. Who is responsible for what happens? God? The devil? Life? Or the one who sows the seed? The harvest can only come from a seed. The field only responds to the seed put into it. So the farmer needs to plant seeds only for what he wants.

If this principle is true for the farmer, then isn't it true for us also? This same principle is true for life in general. If you are getting anything you do not want, or if you have anything in your life right now you do not desire, then my advice to you is to start planting seeds for what you want. And Jesus told us that prayer and faith are involved.

> *"Therefore I say to you, whatever things you ask when you pray, believe that you receive them, and you will have them."* (Mark 11:24 NKJV)

> *"Listen to me! You can pray for anything, and if you believe, you will have it."* (Mark 11:24 NLT 1996)

What are the things you are praying for? The things you want! The law of sowing and reaping teaches where results come from. The law of faith shows you how to reap good in your life.

Three Supernatural Seeds

What are the seeds that make up your belief?

Jesus revealed the three seeds we are to sow for us to have what we want and to remove the mountains in our lives that we do not want. He revealed that mountains and desires both respond to our beliefs.

What you say is a seed.

What you think is a seed.

What you feel strongly (or believe) is a seed.

Now we must look at the seeds we have been given. Once we understand that our seed is what we will see in tomorrow's harvest, we will stop wasting time trying to figure out what will happen tomorrow. The future is what we sow for. This removes the foundation for failure in our lives. It also does not allow us to make excuses for our situation based on what the government is doing or not doing for us. It does not permit us to blame our bad circumstances on a lousy economy, bad parents, bad friends, or a bad environment. We do not blame; we bless. We do not cry; we create. We do not wait; we win. We do not tolerate; we triumph. We do not just exist; we excel.

Most times when negative circumstances come we want to blame someone or something else. The Apostle Paul had to really stress that we must not let ourselves be fooled, because we are not fooling our Creator. Let's look at Galatians 6:7 in three translations.

> *"Don't be misled. Remember that you can't ignore God and get away with it. You will always reap what you sow!"* (NLT 1996)

> *"Don't be misled: No one makes a fool of God. What a person plants, he will harvest."* (Message)

> *"Do not be deceived, God is not mocked; for whatever a man sows, that he will also reap."* (NKJV)

The Law of Faith

> *"Where is boasting then? It is excluded. By what law? Of works? No, but by the law of faith"* (Rom. 3:27 NKJV).

Laws are designed for good. They are intended to protect us. When an offender breaks the law, we want him in jail. There are laws in every area of creation, both seen and unseen. For example, there are laws that govern nature, such as the law of gravity. We build our science on laws that work. In physics, for instance, there are laws that dictate how electricity works. These laws always existed. When men understood them, they could harness the power of electricity for good to bless mankind. But if these laws are broken, then what was meant for good can do evil to you. The same heat generated by electricity to cook eggs on your stove will also cook you if you sit on your stove, even though you are the owner of your stove. The laws that govern electricity are not respecters of persons.

In the same way, the law of faith is a dynamic given for the good of mankind to bring the blessings of heaven to earth. It is the currency of heaven. It is the evidence of things not seen. It is the victory that overcomes the world. It is the answer to all things desired. It is what makes possible the things that look impossible. We can value it for our benefit, or it can easily be used for our destruction. Let us operate in the light of the faith revelation.

What is our future? If we really believed that what we plant today is what we will see tomorrow, then we would start planting what we want to see. What are the seeds that we have to plant? The law of sowing and reaping shows us that good and bad are the result of what we sow. If we want good in our life, Jesus told us very clearly what the seeds are when He revealed the law of faith. Faith is designed to bring to pass good desires, or what you want. If you are not admiring your life right now, then change the seeds you are sowing.

Jesus reveals how to receive what you want.

*"So Jesus answered and said to them, 'Have faith in
God [have the God-kind of faith]. For assuredly, I say
to you, whoever says to this mountain, "Be removed
and be cast into the sea," and does not doubt in his
heart, but believes that those things he says will be
done, he will have whatever he says. Therefore I say
to you, whatever things you ask when you pray, believe that you receive them, and you will have them.'*
"[171]

Jesus used the fig tree to teach humanity this second law,
"the law of faith." It is designed to enable us to receive
God's good and perfect will. This law is built on the first
law of sowing and reaping. It reveals what the good seeds
are and how to sow them so that we will see the harvest
we want in life. It mixes three key ingredients into a very
powerful creative blend that brings everything good and
desirable to us.

Based on this scripture, it is easy to see that **the first seed
of your future is what you are saying** about what you
want. Words are energizers that activate you and others.
When you speak, you energize the atmosphere and the spiritual realm as well. Jesus said that doubt can stop what you
are saying from happening. Doubt originates in your mind;
there is no doubt in a born-again spirit. Doubt must be a
thought process. Because of that, **the second seed must
be what you are thinking** on a regular basis about what
you want. **The third seed is what you are believing.**

How do we comprehend or identify what we believe? Isn't
it true that when we believe something, we have a strong

---

[171] Mark 11:22–24 NKJV

feeling about it? We call that feeling a conviction. It is not a casual opinion but a strong, convinced position. When we have a strong feeling that what we believe is happening, then we could say that **what we feel strongly about— our desire—is our third seed**.

According to this seed concept, *our life is the result of the seeds we have planted.* **The seeds for our life are what we have said, thought, and felt strongly about.**

Seed 1.   The Seed of Saying

"I say to you, whoever says to this mountain . . ." (Mark 11:23 NKJV).

The first thing your words are doing is causing faith to come. If we can't say it, we do not really believe it. Many things we think about die in our thought life. But when we give voice to them they take on a life of their own. Words paint pictures, and those pictures become our realities. The Apostle Paul told us that the miracle life of Christ comes into us when we confess Him as Lord (Rom. 10:9–10). This holy, righteous, victorious life is not in us because we read about it, think about it, or have a family that has it. We experience this life when we decide to accept it in our heart and confess it with our mouth. Each of us possesses the power of choice to determine our future. We might feel controlled right now by other people, physical pain, or economic conditions, but our future is still in our mouths. As Paul said, *"We, having the same spirit of faith, according as it is written, I believed, and therefore have I spoken; we also believe, and therefore speak"* (2 Cor. 4:13).

When I was a tennis pro and instructor some years ago, one of my students was the famous founder of Applied Kinesiology, Dr. George Goodheart. He started to share with me about a new discovery he was working on in his practice. He said that he was observing a connection between health and sounds, and he was very excited about a voice-and-sounds analysis. I told him that was an old discovery given centuries ago, and He stood in shock when I quoted the Bible verse: *"Death and life are in the power of the tongue: and they that love it shall eat the fruit thereof"* (Proverbs 18:21). He had never heard this idea and wanted to stop the tennis lesson for a Bible lesson on this subject, and that's what we did. I do not anticipate this spiritual truth to ever be accepted by natural sciences, but those who are spiritual should be able to see it.

Do we believe what we say?

What makes us unique like our Creator is our ability to transmit pictures or images through the spoken word, to change the seen world with unseen words. As Christians, we believe what we say when we are confident that our words are rooted in the knowledge of redemptive reality. When we know who Jesus is, we know who we are. And when we know who we are, we know what we can do. This is why mountains, obstacles, troubles, and anything else that keeps us from being the best that God made us to be can be removed when we speak.

Do words have creative force? Yes. God used them to create the earth when He said, *"Let there be . . . ,"* and it became. Jesus believed His words had creative power when He said, *"The words that I speak unto you, they are spirit, and they are life"* (John 6:63).

Can His words in our mouths be just as creative? Yes! Jesus said that they surely will be evaluated when we see Him face to face. Our words will justify us or condemn us when we stand before God (Matt. 12:37). The truth that Jesus has given us to speak is so strong and compelling that Jesus said the world will follow Him when we open our mouths and speak. Paul put it this way: *"It pleased God by the foolishness of preaching to save them that believe"* (1 Cor. 1:21).

During much of the first century after Jesus rose from the dead, there was no written Word. At that time He was revealing Himself greatly through the spoken word of His followers. Before He ascended into heaven Jesus told His disciples, *"'Go into all the world and preach the Gospel to every creature'"* (Mark 16:15 NKJV). At the end of that chapter we read that the Lord worked with them and confirmed the Word with signs following (v. 20). The NIV 1984 actually says, *"The Lord worked with them and confirmed His word."* That is still the plan, but it is a lot easier for us today! When God's Word and your words agree, then signs are following you everywhere you go. Now God has His written Word to communicate His plan, personality, and redemptive purpose to all.

Libraries are full of books that are rarely read after the month of their printing. But God's Word carries His very life in it and speaks in a fresh way to every generation. He has given us something to say that we can believe in. Our attitude toward His written Word really determines how much of Him we will experience in our everyday lives. His written Word is a treasure beyond all the riches of this earth. It is designed by God to take the place of Jesus in His absence. It connects us with His thought process. It never sleeps, nor does it ever change its message.

What is our potential in Christianity? It is revealed in Scripture. It is what the Word says about Redemption, the

Body of Christ, and the new creation. We become Christ-like to the degree that we assimilate God's Word into our thoughts and behavior. The Word is Christ revealed. It is His voice and His last message.

What will give you confidence to speak to mountains? Speaking to them the way Jesus did. Only God's living Word on lips of faith can take the place of an absent Christ.

What you say is the picture, goal, and substance of what you are expecting to see from God.

Jesus gave a Roman centurion, a man who had no covenant with God, a higher compliment than He gave to any of God's covenant people. Jesus told His disciples He had not seen greater faith in all of Israel than what He saw in this man (Matt. 8:10). What caused this centurion to receive such a compliment from God? He had evaluated the similarity of authority that he and Jesus carried and told Jesus to speak the Word only, and his servant would be healed.

This soldier's understanding of how his own word of authority operated in the natural realm gave him perfect understanding of how Jesus' words operated in the spiritual realm. This centurion had a revelation that words controlled both realms! If that is the case—and Jesus has given us the keys of the Kingdom of Heaven (Matt. 16:19)—then what we say is the road map to our future. We are our own prophet; we declare our own future.

Can this power be abused? Yes. But it was intended to be used by people with a new, God-filled heart to bring about the desires of that heart.

Proclaiming what you believe is a reasonable step toward seeing what you say.

Paul said, *"I believed, and therefore have I spoken"* (2 Cor. 4:13). If we are smart, what we are saying is either what we are convinced of now, or what we want to be our conviction. Like the rudder of a ship, our words are designed to lead us to our final destination. That destination is not determined by the water, the wind, a map, or the ship. The place we end up is where we set the rudder to take us.

> *"Look also at ships: although they are so large and are driven by fierce winds, they are turned by a very small rudder wherever the pilot desires. Even so the tongue is a little member and boasts great things"* (James 3:4–5 NKJV).

We are overcomers in this life by the blood of the Lamb and the word of our testimony (Rev. 12:11). In His teaching in Mark 11:23–25, Jesus was revealing to us how to use word seeds to move away the mountains in our lives that we don't want, and bring to us what we desire.

Seed 2. The Creative Mind

". . . and does not doubt in his heart" (Mark 11:23 NKJV).

Scientific research over the last 30 years has found that the brain is the largest gland in the body. It releases at least a thousand chemicals into the body at different times, and the depth of its effect on the body is still not completely known.

Even in the natural process of healing our thought life plays a direct role in the chemicals released into the rest of the body. Certain thoughts can be toxic killers if allowed to make deep ruts in our thinking. Lust, anger, hatred, envy, and jealousy are all strong thought patterns.

Thoughts can be deadly. The Scriptures warn that in the last days men's hearts will fail them for fear. The increase in heart attacks in this generation is probably due to the stress, worry, anxiety, fears, and negative information we allow ourselves to dwell on all day long. We have a choice. We can choose to replace thoughts of doubt in our hearts with positive ideas, dreams, and good, pleasant, and lovely reports.

God did not create us to be indoctrinated, but to think. When I was in Bible school, we each had to give a speech before we graduated. One student stood behind the pulpit and declared that everything he was about to say was the exact word of God. He said he had fried his brain cells with drugs, so his brain did not get in the way of his spirit. Soon after that he was kicked out of school!

We have been given the power to think. This power of thought and reason is not a New Age mental exercise. It is a gift from God to understand, formulate, and express our love, our choice, and our fellowship with Him.

> *"Finally, brethren, whatsoever things are true, whatsoever things are honest, whatsoever things are just, whatsoever things are pure, whatsoever things are lovely, whatsoever things are of good report; if there be any virtue, and if there be any praise, THINK ON THESE THINGS"* (Phil. 4:8).

There is a world of possibility surrounding us each day. Beauty and peace can be our continual feast. All we need are eyes to see how God's unmerited favor is now flowing to us, even if we are currently in a terrible situation. *We are called to roll up our sleeves and put our minds in gear. Peter said the following: "Therefore gird up the loins of your mind, be sober, and rest your hope fully upon the grace that*

270

is to be brought to you at the revelation of Jesus Christ."[172]
Loins are the reproductive area of our bodies. Our minds are where thought processes are happening all the time. Our thoughts are from the heart. Solomon told us to guard our hearts with all diligence, for out of the heart flow the issues of life.[173] Doesn't that mean that our thoughts are productive?

Male reproduction produces seeds. Female reproduction provides a birthing place for those seeds. Our minds work in a similar way with our thoughts. The powerful loins of our mind work day and night thinking, imagining, and dreaming about what no one else can see. We should recognize this creativity that is going on in us and do something about it.

We are to gird up the loins of our minds. That means we are to control them or prepare them for action. How? By putting good thoughts in and thinking on the good we want to have and do in the future. We are to create possibilities in our hearts and see the beauty of life. What God did with our spirits is perfect, holy, righteous, and complete, because we are born again of incorruptible seed. But what we do with our thoughts is left to us. Paul told us not to be conformed to this world, but to be transformed by the renewing of our minds (Rom. 12:2). The advertising and news industries are designed to capture our thoughts and direct them. The people who work in those industries understand that if we pay attention to something long enough, we will desire and act on what we think about. Our freedom can be lost when we lose control of our thought life.

---

[172] 1 Peter 1:13 NKJV
[173] Prov. 4:23

I believe I was born again in the basement of a Roman Catholic church in 1974 during the Catholic charismatic renewal. But that one-time decision was never built upon. The new feeling left soon afterward because no knowledge was ever given to me of the spiritual change that had occurred. I asked for a book, but none was given. My mind was full only of the world. That is why I strongly believe in books like this to help people develop a victorious foundation in the new life that is freely given them in Christ. Many years passed before I made another decision for Christ, but that time knowledge helped me to continue on.

Do You Have a Mind for It?

The devil is not able to come into your room in the middle of the night and destroy you or your family. He is limited because he is a loser. So why do we read on the internet and on the front pages of newspapers about foolish, destructive behavior from successful businessmen, politicians, and ministers? The devil didn't make them do it; they entertained and yielded to devilish thoughts.

Solomon penned that above all we should guard our hearts, for out of them flow the issues of life. Life comes from the inside. Nothing changes on the outside until we change on the inside.

People spend their lives offended at what other people did to them, instead of concentrating on the real wealth inside them that could change the world. Paul told us, *"Don't copy the behavior and customs of this world, but let God transform you into a new person by changing the way you think. Then you will know what God wants you to do, and you will know how good and pleasing and perfect his will really is."*[174]

Why does God tell you to do this? Because eventually, whatever goes into your inside will affect your outside. Physically, you may have the desire to look like someone on the front page of a glamour magazine. But you also might have the desire to eat ten hamburgers and a pound of french fries a day. What you put inside of you will eventually show up on the outside and override any higher goal you might have had inwardly.

The gateway to the heart is the mind. When Jesus gave us the key of the power of faith that unlocks success for every person, He said it would work if there was no doubt in our hearts. He was saying that our thoughts must be engaged with our words. Words are required to activate faith, but thoughts are required to sustain our faith so we can attain our goals in life.

Seed 3. Feeling Strongly About Something

"'Therefore I say to you, whatever things you ask when you pray, believe that you receive them, and you will have them'" (Mark 11:24 NKJV).

How do FAITH and FEELINGS work together?

Faith does not rely on feelings, but it absolutely does foster them. Faith does not negate feelings when we talk on the important subject of seeds that produce a result. It is what we feel strongly about that happens in our lives. Only in

---

[174] Rom. 12:2 NLT 1996

the realm of strong conviction can we weather storms that arise. Our beliefs and our strong feelings must be intertwined to form a powerful seed.

I've heard a good definition of strong feelings described as passion. Passion is a mixture of what a person loves and what he hates. Sometimes it's a love of something that drives his passion to change the world, but at other times, it's what angers or disappoints him about the world that leads to a passion to change it. All great achievements must be maintained through passion; otherwise, criticisms, setbacks, and pressures will eventually wear achievers down. In order for passion to exist you must be burning with an idea, or a problem, or a wrong that you want to right. Without passions you will never stick it out when the going gets tough. It's passion that keeps you going in the face of insurmountable odds, and it is the same passion that keeps one refusing to quit no matter how painful the journey to the top is. It is the energy that commits to a goal and stays with it.

True faith is based on the foundation of the known will of God in Scripture. But when we know God's will, we will very often face the worst of storms in how we temporarily feel. Negative feelings of fear, depression, failure, weakness, and malaise that may arise from delayed answers to prayer can hinder our future more than an army of soldiers if we do not deal with them.

We see this operation of faith in the life of Peter. He seems like an unlikely person to be chosen as leader, but he exhibited extraordinary faith. When Jesus was walking on the water in the middle of the storm, Peter did not invite Him into the boat like the other disciples. Peter was willing to do what Jesus was doing–walk on water.

This is the type of faith that makes leaders. It requires two things: keeping your eyes focused on Jesus, and keeping your thoughts off of the circumstances you are in. Peter could not change the water nor the storm, but it did not matter if he could keep his eyes focused and could keep his thought process clear. We can only control what we see and what we think. If what we feel is driven by our circumstances we will never see the results of faith we want. We will stay in the doubt boat and play it safe.

Jesus addressed the feelings of His followers as much as He addressed their faith. He had to deal constantly with fear-based humanity. Walking on the stormy sea, He said to His disciples in the boat, *"Be of good cheer"* (Matt. 14:27). Their emotions were out of control. They were frozen with fear as their eyes looked at the high, destructive seas and saw what they thought was a ghost.

What you focus on is what comes to be in your life. What you view is what you are drawn to. Peter overcame the fear-filled boat by viewing Jesus and acting on His word, and Peter walked on water. For a moment he was the happiest man alive—until he put his eyes back on the waves, and fear regained its grip on his heart.

Another time Jesus told a paralyzed man who was laid at His feet to be of good cheer (Matt. 9:2). That's not what the paralyzed man was looking for. Why did Jesus say it? To move the man's mental focus off of his physical condition and onto a bigger truth to be happy about: his sins were forgiven.

Finding something to be happy about is important if you want change. Joy is a strong feeling of the heart. In this very negative world where negative information touches

you daily, joy must be encouraged, protected, and culti-
vated. When the Apostle Paul was in Jerusalem he was
thrown into jail. Jesus appeared to him there, but not to
deliver him. There was no open door as there had been for
Peter. There was no shaking of the jail as had happened
before. What message did Jesus use to bring Paul through
this difficult time? He told Paul to be of good cheer! Paul
must appear before Caesar.

You might feel as if you are in a financial or physical prison right now, but Jesus is saying, "Be of good cheer! I am
with you in this place." Paul wrote, *"Faith comes by hearing, and hearing by the word of God"* (Rom. 10:17 NKJV).
But he also learned that faith springs from a deep fellowship with the Lord. That fellowship produced an intimacy
that could carry him joyfully across the difficult moments.
Notice that Jesus did not immediately unlock the prison
doors. Jesus was saying to him, "In prison, I will be your
friend, your joy, and your confidence." Your witness must
be protected. Your testimony of the saving, loving, healing
Lord is what Jesus needs in the earth. We do not ignore
the written Word. We confirm with our strong feelings of
faith that it works today. Jesus knew the importance of
knowing Scripture. After His resurrection He had some
strong words for the disciples He met on the Emmaus road.
They did not see how He had fulfilled the Scriptures, and
He had to review for them all that was written about His
death and resurrection: *"And beginning at Moses and all
the prophets, he expounded unto them in all the scriptures
the things concerning himself"* (Luke 24:27).

After Jesus left these two disciples suddenly, they said to
each other, *"Did not our hearts burn within us as He talked
to us and opened the scriptures to us?"* (v. 32). The Word
brings with it a burning vibrancy, a joy, and an expecta-

tion. The Word brings a picture of our future success, purpose, and courage. It is the launching pad from which we go after the desires of our heart. We must foster the strong feelings it generates as positive seeds planted for the harvest of our future.

Is it possible that time can dampen the joy and expectation of an active faith? Can the authority of scripture be diminished and replaced by bad experiences or personal negative feelings? When these experiences do not match up with the model and example of Jesus' ministry do we take Christ out of Christianity? Has the ideal bowed its knee to the experience? Christianity soon moves from an emphasis on living miracle faith to a focus on moral behavior. It tries to produce good people, but they lack power.

The power of your dream, desire, want, or request, and the ability to feel strongly about seeing it become a reality will keep it before you. This is what makes the difference between a lost cause and a glorious victory.

My mother told me that when she was young the teachers in her school wanted her to commit to joining a special religious order because her grades were so good. They thought she would be an excellent candidate. She could read and memorize all the words. She was considering it, but one day she was asked if she would die for what she believed. After much thought she decided she would not die for what she had learned. She knew what was written, but it was not producing a strong feeling, conviction, or vision in her for the future. Many years later, at the age of 65, she met Jesus. Then she was ready to die for what she believed.

To better understand believing as strong feelings, we can easily see that what we feel strongly about is what we act on. What we feel strongly about is what we focus our attention on. What we feel strongly about is what we tend to study about and talk about. Because feelings are possibly the strongest seed that you have, it is very important to feel good. Bad feelings are another term for stress, and the physical body cannot handle it. When you feel bad mentally, those feelings will eventually dominate your heart and produce all sorts of ailments.

The Bible tells us that in the last days men's hearts will fail them for fear (Luke 21:26). I see and hear more fear in people in this 21st century than ever before. Fear controls many nations. But we can rise above fear, alarm, panic, worry, anxiety, and nerves with a stronger feeling. For example, the Bible says a merry heart helps and strengthens us. In contrast, a sad heart is like a poison in our system. It weakens all the areas in which we need to be strong. Here are several verses that illustrate these influences.

> *"A merry heart does good, like medicine, but a broken spirit dries the bones"* (Prov. 17:22 NKJV).

> *"A merry heart maketh a cheerful countenance: but by sorrow of the heart the spirit is broken"* (Prov. 15:13).

> *"All the days of the afflicted are evil: but he that is of a merry heart hath a continual feast"* (Prov. 15:15).

A strong feeling of joy is a key to a long and successful life. It should be guarded as you would protect yourself in a car by wearing a seatbelt, or at the dinner table by not eating spoiled food. And you protect your heart by finding things that keep it full, energetic, and happy. *"The joy of the Lord is your strength"* (Neh. 8:10).

The things that we believe are the things we feel strongly about. We strongly connect emotionally with the seeds of what we are saying and thinking. We are not like newspaper reporters just giving the details of a story. We are not like Hollywood critics acting merely as outside observers. No, we have entered into the arena of faith, and we bring to the Lord in prayer our words, thoughts, and strong feelings about what we want to happen. And the Bible says, *"The effectual fervent prayer of a righteous man availeth much"* (James 5:16). The *New Living Translation 1996* says, *"The earnest prayer of a righteous person has great power and wonderful results."*

Notice that fervent, impassioned, enthusiastic prayer is effective! This kind of prayer is engaged in communion with our Lord. This is how it works: when we work together with Jesus to make a future, we have a meeting of the minds on the outcome. This is the privilege we have because we are in the Kingdom of God, and we have the King in us.

The Lord was often moved with compassion. He was also moved with zeal for the house of God. Our passion releases great power to see His Kingdom come on the earth. To believe in your heart means that you are emotionally connected to what you believe is your future. You are not a casual bystander to your future. You are not resigned to fate. Instead, you are impassioned by faith's expectations. You have a picture of your goal, and you are moving toward it.

James says we show our faith by our actions (James 2:18–26). In our great campaigns we have seen over and over that it was *after* a person got up and began to move, talk, see, or hear that symptoms of deafness, blindness, and paralyzing weakness left. In Chaco, Argentina, there was a young man sitting in his wheelchair way out on the very edge of the campaign grounds. When we challenged the people to do what had been impossible for them to do, he slowly pushed himself up, then took 45 minutes to walk to the platform. To my surprise, he did not testify but just walked slowly back. I did not understand it until the next night when he walked up the steps and told everyone of his 30 years of paralysis from polio. When I asked why he did not testify the night before, he said that he felt he could walk on ground but not on steps. He practiced steps during the day so he could testify!

We encourage everyone to act. Move! Stretch! Bend! Walk! Look! Talk! Do something to connect with your desire. My friend, your future is in your hands. God has already cast His vote for you. He paid for it all. He believes in you and is in you to see your miracle come to pass. He had a plan and picture of your destiny from the foundation of the earth. Your faith decision mixed with His wonderful, unmerited, undeserved favor will bring it to pass. It is not based on what life throws at you, and the devil cannot stop you.

As we consider the law of faith, what are we to believe? Are we to believe just that Jesus is good? Are we to believe that whatever happens is what God desires for us? No! Jesus said to use this powerful creative force of faith to *believe you receive* what you desire. He said, *"Therefore I say unto you, whatsoever ye desire* (what things) *when ye pray, believe that ye receive them, and ye shall have them"* (Mark 11:24).

Believe you have it now. Believe you have at this moment what you want. Believe you have it, and you will have it.

Maybe this has never worked for you. Do you feel as if you will always get what you've always gotten? Is there something that is forcing you to have what you've always had? The good news is, you can change the seed you sow and that will change the harvest of your future.

It does not matter how long we have been reaping a bad harvest. One sowing of good seed will change what the field has produced for a thousand years. Financial difficulties, shortages, bad physical symptoms, and other "mountains" may be present, but that's not what we are believing for. We may see these things right now, but we are believing for what we want. And we sow seeds toward what we want by saying what we want, thinking about what we want, and feeling strongly about what we want. What is it that you want?

"Faith is the substance of things hoped for, the evidence of things not seen" (Heb. 11:1).

What other strong feeling should we consider to see faith work?

I believe we all know that PEACE is a feeling of priceless value. You can have everything, but without having peace you cannot enjoy anything.

When we took off on our first journey around the world, we had only one dollar left after all our bills were paid and the tickets were purchased for the first leg to the Philippines. I looked at Leslie and said if she did not want to go it was ok, and if she went I would give her 50 cents (pennies). She took the money and off we went! Our journey still continues after 30 years.

We all would like to see the resources before we take the steps to our Promised Land, but God likes to see the steps before we see the resources. Faith does not wait for feelings, but feelings are not the enemies of faith. Faith does not depend on emotions, as faith does not see current circumstances as fact. We also understand that feelings cannot be the barometer of faith, because they can be stirred up by words, events, or concerns as often as waves from the sea hit the beach. But feelings also were given by God to ride out those waves. We have to anchor our minds to peace and to the call to reach this world.

Scripture says in Isaiah 26:3, *"Thou wilt keep him in **perfect peace**, whose mind is stayed on thee: because he trusteth in thee."*

PEACE IS A FEELING. The spirit we have from God has feelings! It is called the fruit of the Spirit. *"But the **fruit of the Spirit** is love, joy, peace, longsuffering, gentleness, goodness, faith, meekness, temperance: against such there is no law"* (Galatians 5:22-24).

If faith seems unworkable, then lay the right foundation for it to stand on. The fruit of peace is the cornerstone of faith. Inner peace can be helped, but it cannot be overrun or ignored by the volume of your speech. When Jesus sent His disciples out two- by-two into the towns He was going to visit, He told them to find a house with peace, and if not, leave it. (Luke 10:5). Why? Because their work was hazardous and they needed a place where tranquility and creativity could flourish and the signals of God could be heard. Much can spring out of a heart at rest. When Jesus approached His followers, He often said to be at peace. The epistles open up with a salutation of grace and peace. Faith to see the miraculous springs from your inner peace.

How do we hear and have confidence in our path? The Bible says *"Be still, and know that I am God"* (Psalm 46:10). Internal stillness is where answers come from. The world is stirred up. Panic is a common reaction to negative news. In our era of communication and social media the bad news moves quickly and is constant. What happens? Our bodies, minds and emotions get agitated. Decisions made in this state are usually wrong or mistimed.

When you get under stress where do you go? In what state of mind do you hide? We all go somewhere to cope with the unexpected, unwanted, and unfortunate. Jesus gives us a state of peace to stand in. When He was born the angels cried, *"Peace on earth, good will toward men"* (Luke 2:14). He has given a special place of peace to every soul who calls upon His name. He said: *"Peace I leave with you, my peace I give unto you: not as the world giveth, give I unto you. Let not your heart be troubled, neither let it be afraid."* (John 14:27).

Peace of mind that the world gives is short-term at best. Peace that drugs or alcohol will give is temporary. The book of Proverbs even says that for those who have no hope to have a strong drink. I think God knew that people are going to need some relief. People in constant pain without a hope in Christ will do anything for a release. Jesus does say that, *"In the world you will have tribulation but be of good cheer, I have overcome the world"* (John 16:33). He is not surprised or worried about whatever might happen.

He has a place He has designed for you that the world cannot go to when it is stressed, called the place of peace. When you received Him, He brought peace into your life that will never leave you. That feeling of peace always gives you

283

courage to speak to any storm of irritation or agitation. Those who follow Jesus have a continual knowledge that their relationship with God is all they need. It is a safe harbor for all moving in this sea of humanity. In order for faith to work, it must activate through this heart of peace. Faith can't work without a heart of peace and stillness. The areas where your faith works are the areas where you are at rest, tranquil, and untroubled. This faith God has given us is the most powerful force on earth, but it does not work in doubt, fear, worry, or confusion. We keep calm, at rest, in peace, to see the impossible become possible.

What Do Seeds Do?

Seeds grow, multiply, and give back to you more than you planted.

Our lives today are the sum total of our words, thoughts, actions and beliefs (strong feelings). If we do not like our lives, we need to change the seeds we are sowing. It is important to focus on the good in life and what we desire. We are not to give attention to tribulation, trial, or lack unless we want tribulation, trials, and lack in our life.

What you pay attention to is what increases in your life. Whatever you give consideration to will increase, whether it is good or bad. This is why we are told over and over in the Scriptures not to worry, fret, or have anxiety about anything, but to trust in God. I will say it again—our physical body is not designed to handle too much stress. We are designed to live fear-free and stress-free.

What are we to do with our time? We are to talk about what we want and give attention to what we desire to see as our future. We are to use our power of choice to choose a good result and keep our focus on it. How long do we look to the good? We must look long enough to allow time to develop a picture in our inner man of a good, guilt-free, condemnation-free new person. That new person is full of positive feelings about the things desired in life. This is the Godkind of faith in operation. It calls those things that are not as though they are. Having not seen, yet we believe. And the sign of our believing is the joy flowing from our hearts. It is the sign that our faith is working and our seed is developing. The Apostle Peter talked about this.

> *"Jesus Christ: Whom having not seen, ye love; in whom, though now ye see him not, yet believing, ye rejoice with joy unspeakable and full of glory: receiving the end of your faith, even the salvation of your souls."*[175]

This excites me because all people of the earth have the right to plant faith seeds for results. When we travel the earth preaching these dynamic truths, it provides a permanent source of life, health, freedom, and supply for people. It is infinitely better than any government seed program, even though we appreciate their efforts.

Faith dynamics in prayer are not limited to one people, group, denomination, nationality, or color. Whoever dares to pray in faith will see the same results as in Bible days, wherever they may be and whenever they choose to step out. Your discovering the law of faith is like Columbus discovering the New World. It opens up a new realm of possibility. It is like the Wright brothers discovering the man-made flight. It lifts you to a new perspective where you can see as far as you want to see!

---

[175] 1 Peter 1:7–9

The next two pages contain manifestos that will help build into your daily thinking the transforming power of the dynamic concepts I have mentioned in this book. When they come alive in you, you can produce the kind of miracle life you have dreamed of!

Read them aloud often. You may see results in a few months, or you might need a year. Even if it takes a while, stay with it. In a year you will not recognize the new and wonderful you!

MY MIRACLE MANIFESTO
DECLARATION OF WHO I AM

Lord Jesus,

You revealed God in human flesh and now you reveal Yourself in my flesh.

The love, forgiveness, and supernatural life of healing and miracles you demonstrated in the Gospels is now what You demonstrate in my life, as I continue what the Book of Acts started after Your resurrection from the dead. The new era with the new way of life revealed in the Gospels is now authenticated in my life. The authority recognized by the spirit realm in Your life, is now the authority recognized as I speak in Your name. Devils knew who You were and bowed their knee. Now devils recognize You in me as Your representative and bow their knee. Jesus, the Word was alive and productive on Your lips, and now Your Word is alive and productive through me. I do not beg for what You have accomplished. I communicate and demonstrate what you have finished and freely given. You took my sin and gave me a clean start. You took my sickness and gave me a sound body. You took my pains and gave me relief.

You took my death and gave me life. You took my disease and gave me Your health. You took my weakness and gave me Your strength. You took my doubts and gave me faith. You took my grief and gave me joy. You took my judgment and gave me a righteous position in life. Now I have the power to continue in excellence all You began. Now I continue to experience Jesus alive in me.

288

I continue to educate all of hurting humanity. I continue to expect answers to my prayers. I continue to stay up in a down world. Jesus, I see You in life as my example. I see You in death as my substitute. I see You in hell overcoming the devil. I see You risen overcoming death. I see You in me reigning in life.

DECLARATION OF WHAT I CAN DO

Lord Jesus,

You have taken me from just being a spectator in life to fully participating. Because I know who I am and who You are in me, I am no longer on the sidelines of just reporting, criticizing, or sitting on the fence. I have entered into the arena of life!

Jesus, You were born of a virgin. Now I am born of Your incorruptible seed—Your Word. You lived a sinless life. Now I have had my sins blotted out by Your blood sacrifice, and I no longer live conscious of my sins and shortcomings.

The very blood of God the Creator and my Father flowed in Your veins. You shed that blood to redeem me and qualify me to live a new life with my slate clean from all the mistakes, sins, and failures of the past. As a result of discovering who You are, I discover what You have done for me, and now, what You are doing through me. You were with my Father in the very beginning and have known me from the foundations of the earth. By faith in Your resurrection life in me, I am raised from the dead, and I live victoriously over Satan, devils, and all works of destruction. Now I live free of guilt, shame, and inferiority. I am infused with Your Spirit, and I am able to do as You have done.

I am a continuer of all that You began to do. Your miracle life is unlocked in me as I allow You to work through me, and I speak Your Word of life. As You showed the Father to the world, now I show You to the world. As the Father has sent You, now You send me.

The works that You did as an example to Israel, You now do through me as a demonstration to the world. I represent You on earth, even as You represented Father God on earth. What You were in a Jewish body 2,000 years ago, You are in my body today!

You have called me from my mother's womb and have entrusted Your glorious Gospel to me. You believe in me, You trust me, You love me. You believe I can do what is in my heart and what is in Your Word. What You began I will continue because You live in me and confirm what I say when I speak Your ideas. Only by my deeds are Your seeds sown into the earth. I am filled with Your Holy Spirit Who has empowered me to be Your witness. Now I am appointed, anointed and equipped to represent You wherever I go. I am following You by being a fisher of men and women. I DARE TO SHARE BECAUSE I CARE ABOUT PEOPLE!

Jesus, You saved me and made me a messenger of salvation. You healed me and made me a healer. You lifted me and made me a lifter. You delivered me and now You deliver others through me.

CONCLUSION
WHAT DID YOU DISCOVER IN THIS BOOK?

Now that you have read this book, I believe that you have seen enough to take your seat of highest privilege—The 12th Chair at God's table. And I believe that the miracle life that Jesus modeled for us has become your blueprint for living. You have begun your journey to the life of miracles that the Scriptures call us to walk in!

In this book, we have sought answers to big questions about our potential. Who are we because of Jesus? What do we have because of Him? What can we do through Him? I believe that this quest has stimulated a hunger in you to know and understand more about who God has created you to be. Real life lies within us, and tapping into that Miracle Life has been our goal.

God has given us the privilege of representing Jesus. Without us, God cannot accomplish His will in the earth. And without Him, we cannot realize our purpose! We need each other. Through us, God is fulfilling His desire to have a family. His will is that no one perish but that all should be saved.[176] Tragically, some will not listen.

Jesus is training us the same way He trained His first disciples. He is taking us from revelation to revelation, and from experience to experience so we can see Him, His truth, and a demonstration of His presence wherever we go.

---

[176] John 3:16

We have seen that Jesus is the same today in His Word as He was 2,000 years ago in His flesh. And we've discovered that God's Spirit in us in the 21st century is the same as God's Spirit in Jesus in the 1st century.

This reality sets Jesus apart from all other spiritual leaders of history. It makes Him unique. His Word is credible and can be validated. This brings the spiritual and natural worlds together.

Jesus' resurrection means our limited life now has the touch of the unlimited. The results of our natural efforts become supernatural when we act like Him!

Religion has asked us to settle for less than this type of life. However, Jesus is calling us to experience life on earth the way He experienced it. Doing this will put freshness into each day! It will put an attitude of expectation in our hearts and a joyful sound in our voices!

Do you know what inspires you—what excites you so that you are not living a boring, legalistic, religious life? *"Unlimited Inspiration,"* the next book in the series, will explore ways to stay up in a down world. It will show you how to continue what Jesus began and not fall into expecting less of life.

"Unlimited Inspiration" will give you a treasure chest of reasons for living high on life—full of expectation! It will straighten your backbone and encourage you to reach your potential. As you read this book, you will awaken to your greatest goals, stand in your redemption, and *go* with excitement and passion to a world eagerly waiting to receive you!

When you finish reading *"Unlimited Inspiration,"* you will have a new spring in your step and a vision for the future larger than you ever dreamed! I am fully persuaded that this book series will produce new life, confidence, purpose, health, hope, and prosperity in you as you connect with God's best! So join the adventure that takes you to greater heights of living in Jesus Christ.

Don't hitch your salvation to an assumption!

Can there be a more important decision than the one that determines where we spend eternity? Every other decision seems trivial at best when compared with this one. Yet billions, myself included, have made assumptions about salvation that we would never make about any other decision!

Here are three mistakes you can make:

1. Not reading the contract for yourself. For 22 years I assumed that the leader of my church had everything under control. He read the contract for us and told us what to do. He read it but never signed it himself or had any of us sign it. We were never told what was required to guarantee a relationship with God and ensure us a place in heaven.

2. Not understanding the conditions. I was told I was a good guy, so I assumed I was going to heaven. I presumed that was enough. Millions of people compare themselves with others and believe they are not so bad, so they think they will make it to heaven. I belonged to a big church, so I supposed they could not all be wrong. I thought my church membership would get me in! This is folly. Without a relationship with the living God, you cannot be sure that you are going to heaven.

3. Not knowing a clear path to God exists. My last assumption was that no one could personally know for sure where he or she would spend eternity. Now I realize that if you do not know, you will not go! My greatest moment in life came under an maple tree at Michigan State University in June of 1978. That's when I made my connection with God. For the first time I knew my past was forgiven and my future in heaven was secure. If I never knew anything else, that alone was enough to enable me to die a happy man!

There is a choice to make.

The power of choice determines your future. Even though God loves you and has provided for you a wonderful life on earth and one in the time to come, *accepting* what He has provided is still your choice. Even though He knew you before you were born and provided a purpose and provision for your life, He cannot choose that for you. You must choose it for yourself.

There is a heaven to gain and a hell to avoid in everyone's future. Hell was never intended for people. It was designed for devils who willfully chose to reject God.

This body we live in is temporary, but our spirit is eternal and it will live in either heaven or hell forever. You are a unique person, but you are not the first person born on the earth, and you cannot make the rules.

When we were born, we entered a human drama that has continued from creation until now. In this drama, men and women were separated from their Creator when they deliberately rejected His words. God made mankind in His image and breathed a part of Himself into us, giving us nobility, dignity, authority, and the right to accept or reject

Him. When the first man, Adam, rejected God's words, he rejected God, and sin became man's new nature. Rejecting God separated mankind from their Creator.

But the Creator's nature is love, and love made a way to receive back any person who would choose to walk with Him. He did it by sacrificing His Son, Jesus Christ. Jesus came to earth to reveal the true God to people and restore their connection with Him. Jesus revealed who God is and who we are, and then He died in our place on a cross to pay the price for our wrongs. Because Jesus laid down His life as a love offering, we are redeemed—brought back to God our Creator. And we can stand before Him without shame, guilt, or sin—just as Adam did when he was first created!

This is the real "new birth." It is available to every individual who will hear the truth about it, believe it, and receive the Savior, Jesus Christ. When you do this, your old sin nature is replaced with God's Spirit and His right nature. You are born again! You become one of a new species of being on the earth—without sin but with the nature of God. That is what qualifies you to go to heaven and avoid hell.

Once you are born again, hell cannot receive you because you are a child of God. There is no place in hell for those born of God, and there is no place in heaven for those who are not. Scripture tells us that those who call upon Jesus as their Savior have their names written in the Book of Life.[177] They have made a covenant with God that is signed in the blood of Jesus Christ!

Jesus chose to fulfill the Creator's will and take your place in being punished for sin. When you choose to accept Jesus as your Savior, you satisfy the requirement to get into heav-

---

[177] Phil. 4:3

en. And God, faithful to His Word, replaces the sin-fallen spirit within you with a clean, holy, righteous spirit without sin and ready for heaven.

God has no grandchildren, He only has children. Each of us must decide for ourselves what to do with Jesus and where we will spend eternity. The Apostle Paul said we activate salvation with our heart and our mouth. Salvation that comes from trusting Christ—which is the message we preach—is within easy reach. Scripture tells us,

> *"'The message is very close at hand; it is on your lips and in your heart.' And that message is the very message about faith that we preach: If you confess with your mouth that Jesus is Lord and believe in your heart that God raised him from the dead, you will be saved. For it is by believing in your heart that you are made right with God, and it is by confessing with your mouth that you are saved."*[178]

"For the Scripture says, 'Whoever believes in him will not be disappointed.' "[179]

Put your heart and mouth into action now!

Seize this moment by praying to God. He is not far from you, and He is true to His Word. When you accept Jesus as Lord, God will confirm your decision by making His presence real in you. It was His idea to get you back. It was His idea to send the Savior. It was His idea to live in you. Express your need to Him and receive your Savior today by praying this out loud. God will honor your prayer and your choice:

---

[178] Rom. 10:8–10 NLT
[179] Rom. 10:11 NASB

297

"Lord Jesus,

I recognize my condition. I am a sinner, disconnected from God the Father and from You. I am guilty of sin, and I am not sure where I will spend eternity. I have lived long enough without You. I am taking a step toward You now and thank You for taking a step toward me. I believe that You died for my sins and You rose from the dead, and that You are alive forever. Now I ask You to come into my heart. Thank You for washing me clean right now. You said all who call upon You will be saved. I trust You with my life and my future. By faith I say what Your Word says—that I am a new person. I am born again, not of earthly seed but of eternal seed. Heaven is *now* my home! Thank You, Jesus, for taking away my sin and making me new. You are my Savior and Lord!

Amen."

Jesus said:

> *"Verily, verily, I say unto you, He that heareth my word, and believeth on him that sent me, hath everlasting life, and shall not come into condemnation; but is passed from death unto life."*[180]

WELCOME TO GOD'S FAMILY!

---

[180] John 5:24

Other Books By Kevin & Leslie McNulty

UNLIMITED INSPIRATION
Tap into the limitless resource within you. Discover the keys to continue the miracle life of Jesus. Discover A CONTINUAL SOURCE OF MOTIVATION.

HIGH ADVENTURES IN CHRISTIAN LIVING
Unique adventure. It will stir you to new exploits in your daily life.

RIVER AND RAIN
Discover a place where you are not dependent on the government, the economy, the mercy of others or your own manipulations. God deposited in you the power to produce wealth just as surely as He deposited the power of eternal life in you.

YOU CAN DO IT eBook
Helps new converts in their first steps of Christianity, giving quick and clear insights to being born again, healed and spirit-filled.

PATHWAY TO YOUR HEALING eBook
Is healing more difficult to receive than salvation?
What are the 7 fundamental "Pathways to Your Healing"?

• Go to our website to check our front page articles, photo reports, and read our blogs.

• Become a Monthly Partner – the foundation of the ministry rests on the small $20 gifts of many caring people. The souls saved are directly related to partnership.

• Support an Evangelist – every $100 monthly gift is enough for us to salary an evangelist so his family is provided for as he begins this new, soul-winning effort in virgin territory.

SOCIAL MEDIA INFO
• *Facebook.com/ McNultyMinistries*
• *Twitter.com/drlesliemcnulty or drkevinmcnulty*
• *YouTube.com/mcnultyministries*

ABOUT THE AUTHOR

Dr. Kevin McNulty is a global evangelist, pastor, teacher, author, and diplomat of Christ to presidents and national churches. He is best known for his mass-miracle events and the impact of the 100-Tent Project across Eurasia, which he started with his wife, Leslie, co-founder of Christian Adventures International.

Dr. McNulty has proclaimed the Gospel to millions in more than 60 nations for over 30 years, speaking to crowds of 5,000 to 250,000 during conferences and outdoor events. He lived in Russia for 10 years planting churches and Bible schools and training missionaries. This has given him a unique perspective on today's global environment.

Kevin earned a master's degree and doctorate from Life Christian University and a bachelor's degree from Michigan State University, where he was captain of the Big Ten varsity tennis team.

Drs. Kevin and Leslie McNulty served as International Directors and associate ministers with Dr. T.L Osborn for 16 years. They are also founding members of the Russian Union of Christians of Evangelical Faith; a government recognized Protestant Church organization.

ENDORSEMENTS

My good friend, Dr. Kevin McNulty, has lived a miracle life for over 35 years. I have seen the revelation contained in this book demonstrated in every arena of his life. It's more than theory, for it has been tested on the harvest fields of over 60 nations and has influenced the multitudes.

The 12th Chair contains the seeds for success in life and ministry. It's not a self-help book, but a book of truth that will challenge you to live the miracle life Jesus came to bring. This book will help you discover your purpose and help you to dream again. Let it pump new life into your heart and cause you to take your place in God's family living His miracle life.

Jeff Miller, Pastor of Abundant Life Family Church, Aurora, IL, USA

Dr. Kevin has surpassed any and all expectations with the 12th Chair. This book is filled with insight to a new dimension of spiritual living for the hungry reader. His ability to communicate through words is a powerful gift of God that stirs the human spirit to believe.

Andrew Cunningham, Pastor of SouthGate Church, Phoenix, Arizona, USA

As I read The 12th Chair, I wanted to shout 'Hallelujah'! Dr.McNulty releases the power of God in your life to make you more than a conqueror. Caution: your life is about to be revolutionized.

Ken Eldred, businessman, entrepreneur, and author of God Is at Work

One of the saddest places on the planet is a graveyard. While you may be nodding in agreement and I'm not callous to the emotion, I have an even greater consideration that bothers me. It's the wasted potential embalmed and lying in that grave. Morbid? I guess. But those kind of thoughts have challenged me personally and caused me to bring that challenge to those I influence. I want them to be sure they do all they can to enthusiastically live out their God given potential until their last dying breath.

THE 12th CHAIR (by my friend of three decades, Dr. Kevin McNulty) is a book that will challenge you to sit in the seat that has been reserved for you. It is one of adventure and significance that God intends for every human being to participate in and enjoy. Come on, fill that empty chair! It may not always be the most comfortable seat in the house, but it will always be the most rewarding.

Jerry R. Weinzierl, Pastor of Grace Christian Church, Sterling Heights, Michigan, USA